Herotica

A Collection of
Women's Erotic Fiction
Second Edition

Also by Susie Bright

Herotica 2 (editor, with Joani Blank, NAL/Plume)

Herotica 3 (editor, NAL/Plume)

Susie Sexpert's Lesbian Sex World (Cleis Press)

Susie Bright's Sexual Reality: A Virtual Sex World Reader (Cleis Press)

The Best American Erotica series (editor, Macmillan)

SexWise (Cleis Press)

Nothing but the Girl: The Blatant Lesbian Image (with Jill Posener, Freedom Editions)

Susie Bright's Sexual State of the Union (Simon & Schuster)

Herotica

A Collection of
Women's Erotic Fiction
Second Edition

Introduction and Afterword
by SUSIE BRIGHT, Editor

Down There Press • San Francisco, California

Herotica, second edition, copyright © 1988, 1998 by Susie Bright

Individual contributions copyright ©1988 by their authors

We offer librarians an Alternative CIP prepared by Sanford Berman
of Hennepin County Library.

Alternative Cataloging-in-Publication Data

```
Bright, Susie, editor.
Herotica: a collection of women's erotic fiction. San
Francisco, CA: Down There Press, copyright 1988, 1998.
Twenty-one stories, by Cheryl Cline, Nancy Blackett,
Isadora Alman, Lisa Palac, and others.
1. Women's erotica. 2. Women's fiction, American-20th
Century. 3. Short stories, America-20th Century. 4.
Women-Sexuality-Fiction. 5. Lesbians-Sexuality-
Fiction. 6. Erotica fiction, American-20th Century.
I. Down There Press. II. Title. III. Title: Women's
erotica fiction. IV. Title: Her erotica.      .
813.5408                      F
```

ISBN 0-940208-24-5   LC # 98-72962

Printed in the United States of America   9 8 7 6 5 4 3

Cover Design: Gail Grant

Additional copies of this book are available at your favorite
bookstore or directly from the publisher:

Down There Press, 938 Howard St., #101, San Francisco CA 94103

Please enclose $15.75, which includes $4.75 for shipping/handling.

Please visit our Web page: *www.goodvibes.com/dtp/dtp.html*

Contents

Acknowledgments

My admiration, gratitude and thanks to Joani Blank, Honey Lee Cottrell, and Debi Sundahl for their insight, support, and particular genius which helped me edit and introduce this anthology. Invaluable editorial assistance was provided by Deborah Sachs, Leigh Dickerson Davidson, Elinore Fox and Elena Chieffo.

Introduction

What comes to mind when she shuts her eyes and thinks about sex? What appeals to the female erotic imagination?

Before we can courageously reveal the correct answer to this question, we have to admit it's a tough one. Women's sexual expression has been Top Secret for as long as we've been wondering. It's such a taboo that women themselves don't share with each other what turns them on. Oh sure, you'll get game show confidences that masquerade as women's desires ("Bachelorette Number One, what color eyes really turn you on?"), but to reveal a woman's lust is to admit a sexual power that not everyone is prepared to bite into.

I began my pursuit of women's erotica looking underneath my girlfriends' beds. Stashed away, but within arm's reach, I discovered back issues of "men's" magazines, Victorian-era ribald short stories, trashy novels with certain pages dog-eared, plain brown wrapper stroke books that seemed to have had a previous owner, classics like *The Story of O* or *Emmanuelle*, and even serious critiques of pornography that were paper-clipped to fall open to the "good parts."

Women build their erotica collections in a dedicated but haphazard manner. One friend raided her brother's bedroom in the early 1960s for pulp novels with lesbian themes. Another holds onto a ragged copy of *Valley of the Dolls* because it was the first risque literature she had ever come across. I can remember when all my junior high girlfriends passed around an excerpt from *The Godfather* (the famous pp. 27-28), describing a woman with a large and insatiable vagina who finally meets her match. One plain brown wrapper in my collection came courtesy of a hitchhiker who left his coat in a friend's car with a copy of *Doris and the Dick* in the front pocket. While many women would never walk into a liquor store to purchase a brand new copy of *Penthouse*, there are always garage sales, wastebaskets and back issues from male friends who never notice that the May 1978 issue has disappeared forever from their stacks.

Feminism opened new opportunities for the female pornographic library. On the blatant side were the feminist erotic pioneers, who proudly issued the first volumes of women's sexual points of view. Nancy Friday's successful fantasy revelations (*My Secret Garden, Forbidden Flowers*), Betty Dodson's call to self-orgasm (*Liberating Masturbation*), Tee Corinne's explicit *Cunt Coloring Book*, and Anais Nin's erotic short stories (*Delta of Venus*) appeared. Women finally had a handful of literature that could turn us on. Moreover, we could enthusiastically embrace each author as one of our own.

Another side of the feminist movement in publishing revealed a more devious method for women to discover their prurient interest. If it hadn't been for Kate Millet tearing apart Henry Miller's sexist prose in *Sexual Politics*, a lot of us might never have been initiated into one-handed reading. As anti-porn theoreticians made their case, they cited examples as shocking and outrageous as they could find, apparently disregarding that their audience could be just as easily aroused as offended, and probably both.

Since the late 1970s, both mainstream and underground women's erotica have grown in fits and spurts. On the plus side we have an explosion in X-rated home videos, a whopping 60 percent of which are rented by women. Virtually all these movies are man made, and of moderately to extremely poor quality. Women are exasperated but well-practiced in "taking what I can get and making the best of it." This has been the theme song of women's sexual repression. Subverting men's fantasies and using them for our own arousal is the foundation of every woman's under-the-bed bookshelf.

When women have taken a hand in the production of erotica, the results have been underpublicized and thwarted in distribution, but tremendously rewarding. For the first time, we have women producing diverse, contemporary clit's point-of-view erotica. Note the success of sexual fiction anthologies like *Pleasures, Erotic Interludes* and *Ladies Own Erotica*, of a magazine like the lesbian *On Our Backs*, or women's erotic videos like those of Candida Royalles' Femme Productions and the lesbian video companies Fatale and Tigress.

There's still a lot of confusion about what the label "women's erotica" means. At its worst, it's a commercial term for vapid femininity, a Harlequin romance with a G-string. The very word "erotic" implies superior value, fine art, an aesthetic which elevates the mind and incidentally stimulates the body. "Women's pornography," on the other hand, is a contradiction in terms for many people, so convinced are they that pornography represents the darker, gutter side of lust. We are enmeshed in a semantic struggle for which words will describe our sexual creativity. What turns women on? And why have we been silent on the subject for so long? As we begin to reveal, in detail, the complexity and scope of our sexual desires, the appropriate language will evolve.

I recently saw a bumper sticker that said in plain blue letters: HONOR LUSTFUL WOMEN, and I thought, "Now here's someone who might understand the concept of an earthy woman's erotica or an elegant female pornography."

At least we can get one thing straight before we wander down the path of feminine hedonism: some women want the stars, some the sleaze. Some desire the nostalgia of the ordinary, some the punch of the kinky. And some want all of it. Our sexual minds travel everywhere, and embrace every emotion. Our sexual fiction is not so different from men's in terms of physical content. Its uniqueness lies in the detail of our physical description, our vulnerability and the often confessional quality of our speech in this new territory. Above all, because we have had so little of women's sexual fiction, there is absolutely no formula to follow.

Men's sexual literature has been commercialized and compartmentalized into little catalogs of unvarying formulas. In the same way that women have had to "make do" with men's porn to satisfy their sexual curiosity, men have had to fit the diversity of their experience into the same pair of tight shoes over and over again. The result is some very stubborn callouses. Men have had the Faustian bargain that if they agree to keep their erotic interests out of their family life, and out of the public eye, they can enjoy the privilege of varied and no holds barred voyeurism. But that variety and access only go so far. The embarrassment, shame and double standard that surround men's license to pornography are stifling, and breed cynicism.

Women's sexual fiction is new, it reflects up our skirts (and jeans) like a patent leather shoe, and it squeaks and pinches, drawing out mysteries and unexpected sighs of pleasure.

How can we tell if it's the real thing? Is there any foundation to women's erotica that will define the new breed?

The most obvious feature of women's erotic writing is the nature of the woman's arousal. Her path to orgasm, her anticipation, are front and center in each story. Even if her climax is not part of the scene, it is her sexual banquet that is being served, whether she is the initiator, the recipient, the reciprocator, the voyeur, or the exhibitionist. There are even times when the female reader is drawn to identify with a male character, but it is in the spirit of vicarious interest.

Women's erotica objectifies all the sexual possibilities, which is a more precise way of describing "foreplay." It doesn't matter whether it's describing a lover's body for her own pleasure, or a titillating meal for her consumption. Wake up, class, it's time to redefine "objectification." We're not talking about being chased around the boardroom or accosted in the street. In sexual literature and art, the process of objectification is a very natural and sensitive one. The reader integrates the words and pictures into her own sexual imagination in order to create heat; this means manipulating images for her own pleasure.

Women have not had the chance to do this before, because men were always exposing themselves to us before we had a chance to give them the once over. They had the permission to look, read, and suit themselves — we were told to wait, refrain, and submit to the inevitable.

Women's contribution to erotic objectification has been to expand the territory of compelling sexual possibilities; not only to romanticize, but to virtually fetishize erotic environments. I used to laugh at traditional women's supermarket novels where every chapter is filled with minute details of what the heroine is going to wear next. Now I realize this was a repressed goody-girl version of sexual objectification. Bad girls, as they say, go everywhere, and costuming is just the tip of the iceberg.

So far, women writing erotica have been ambivalent about the responsibility of sexual portrayal. Danger and physical risks are often a part of sexual fantasy, and each female author seems to have a different take on how much reassurance they should give to the reader that this is, after all, fiction. There's a rebellion brewing among female sex writers, because they're desperate to explore sex for sex's sake, not as a health issue. Often they're the same people who have been on the front lines of birth control counseling, or safe sex education. Women writers have been far more prolific about the consequences of irresponsible or harmful sexual behavior than they have been describing either their erotic identities or the brutal consequences of sexual repression: on our health, independence and self-esteem as women.

For *Herotica*, we chose stories which range from fantasy to autobiographical, nostalgic to pressing, quick and dirty to philosophical and maddening. We wanted to reflect the gender blending and role switching that has not been previously acknowledged, but that is certainly a part of most women's fantasy lives. It's often lamented that the categories of straight-gay-bisexual don't do justice to our erotic identities. I believe this collection takes a first step at revealing the multiple dimensions of our sexual character.

What's hot and what's not for the female audience is going to continue to be controversial and late breaking news. We are pioneers not only in putting women's sexuality into overt public consciousness, but also in giving respect and diversity to erotic literacy. With any luck, this anthology will find its place not only under the bed but on a few coffee tables and in a few libraries as well.

Susie Bright, San Francisco, March 1988

Pickup

Cheryl Cline

He was one cute guy, that guy with the pickup. He had come into Sil's bar, Vickie's favorite weekend hangout, a couple three times before Vickie ever got up the nerve to push herself in his direction. This guy was, as her roommate Joan would say, "A fox." Blond hair, black vest, white T-shirt, blue jeans, black boots — *heavy* black boots. Plus a black leather belt and chains that didn't look like they were *for* anything, and a big blue-handled comb sticking up out of his back pocket. You could see each and every tooth on that comb.

He would come in by himself, standing in the doorway a little uncertainly, looking for his bar-buddy, Steve. If he got there before Steve, he'd go back outside and hang around his truck until Steve got there, and then they'd both swagger in, stomp up to the bar and yell "Bud!" If Sherry was tending bar that night, Steve would always and without fail lean over the bar and leer. "You got something I want, babe," he'd say.

"It'll cost ya," Sherry'd throw back at him, clunking down a heavy beer glass and filling it expertly just to the top, never spilling any over the sides. Sherry always gave the guy with the pickup a wink as she slid his beer over the counter, because she liked the way he'd duck his head and give her this shy sort of grin. That thick blond hair of his would fall down into his eyes, and didn't she just want to smooth it back for him.

Beers in hand, he and Steve would head for the jukebox, Steve looking the place over for likely Friday-night girlfriends. The guy with the pickup mainly looked at the floor.

But tonight his eyes flashed towards Vickie as he walked past. They dropped just as quickly, but a second later he looked up again as if to convince himself, hey, she's looking at *me*. The wistful look in his eyes sent a warm hollow feeling right through Vickie. She peered thoughtfully into her glass. Uh-oh.

At the jukebox, the two friends dug deep into their pockets for the first of the night's quarters and argued about what to play. They decided on something loud — they always did. Screaming, driving, noisy stuff, heavy metal, headbanger music that slammed right into the pit of your stomach. The ritual of the jukebox over, they took their beers to a table and sprawled all over a couple of chairs. In a few minutes they were off into some energetic talking, with lots of table-pounding, back-thumping and frequent trips to the bar. Vickie couldn't hear over the blast of the jukebox what they talked about, but it was spiked with "Awww, *man!*" and "Awwwright!" and every few minutes Steve would move into a screaming air-guitar solo.

Once in a while, the guy with the pickup would look over ever-so-casually at Vickie. Whenever he met her eyes, he'd suddenly turn to Steve with some quick joke and punch or kick him or something. Gradually Vickie realized he was trying to catch her attention.

"That guy's looking at you," said Joan matter-of-factly. Joan was looking out for Vickie's interest. The night before at home, Vickie had chopped a big hunk of roast into stew meat while Joan read the personal ads from the *Bay Guardian*.

"Listen here: 'SWM, rock-hard but sensitive, will share membership in posh fitness center with agile woman who likes to get down and get sweaty.' Chi-rist. Oh, here's one: 'SWM desires company of bright woman, 18-25, non-smoking vegetarian, willing to engage in joyous exploration of the overworld as well as the ecstasy of the purely physical.'"

Vickie pushed the meat into a pile and leaned against the sink. "Is there one in there," she said, "that says, 'White guy, Van

Halen fan, works, eats and sleeps in Coors trucker hat, wants cute chick for meaningful relationship in the back of a 1972 Chevy four-wheel drive pickup with overlarge tires and a Harley-Davidson sticker in the back window.'?"

"Oh, yeah, sure." Joan snorted and slapped the edge of the table with the paper. Wistfully contemplating a large bowl of carrots, she said, "Those guys never advertise."

Maybe not, Vickie thought, watching the guy with the pickup. But tonight she was going to answer that ad.

"Do you know who he is?" she asked.

Joan blew smoke through her nose. "Nope. But I *do* know a little bit about the guy he's with. He's a jerk." She gave the men at the table her famous once-over and jerked her thumb at the jukebox. "Couple of rivet-heads."

"I can hear that," said Vickie. "But the blond is kinda cute, don't you think?"

"Oh, sure, he's cute. Loves his mother, probably. Look at those brown doe eyes." She sighed, and rested her chin on her hand. "Probably one of those psychotic killers you hear about."

Vickie laughed. "But his eyes *are* nice."

"Just proves my point — there, now look at him!"

The guy with the pickup had just donned a pair of evil-looking black wraparound sunglasses and was admiring himself in a Schlitz mirror.

"Uh-oh," said Vickie. "Someone's coming." Steve had noticed the women's attention, but mistaking its object, had pushed back his chair and was aiming himself unsteadily in their direction. He prodded the guy with the pickup, but his friend merely smiled and held on to his beer glass like it was going to save him from something.

"Look," Joan stage-whispered. "Leave the beast to me. Here's your chance to swoop down on his friend."

With what she was sure was a fatuous expression, Vickie rose and swerved past Steve just as he reached the bar. He spun halfway round.

"Hey!"

"Hey yourself," she heard Joan say firmly, behind her. Now it was too late to back down. The guy with the pickup had seen her and was looking real casual, tapping the wraparounds on the table, shifting his heavy boots.

Vickie sank down in Steve's vacated chair and on a nervous impulse scooped up the wraparounds and put them on.

"How do I look?" she asked, turning her face this way and that, modeling. The guy with the pickup was silent and Vickie's heart fell. She lowered the sunglasses to the tip of her nose, peered over them, and grinned in relief when she saw him smiling a little lopsidedly and blushing clear to the neck of his white, white T-shirt. He jerked his thumb upwards in approval.

"Awwright!"

Hoo-boy, Vickie thought.

He fell silent, searching for something to say.

"What's your name?" she asked brightly.

"Phil."

Vickie put out her hand. "Pleased to meet you, Phil." He shook her hand solemnly. The two of them made their way awkwardly through a couple of rounds of beer and the usual small talk: What do you do, do you have sisters, where do you live, is the rent high there, mind if I smoke, have you been over to Hobie's yet?

It wasn't too hard to get him to talk, really, though at first he answered questions in monosyllables and kept looking over at Steve as if for help. Vickie was very tactful, careful to act as much the lady as was possible in a place like Sil's, sensing that if she made any too-sudden moves, he'd run to the men's room and not come out. The jukebox screeched to silence and Vickie smiled as Joan beat Steve across the room by a length. Before he could argue, she'd fed in her quarters and punched her buttons, and a few seconds later, the Shirelles took over.

Phil became more animated, and, Vickie was surprised to find, more serious as he talked. He talked about himself, of course — beer will do that — but not the way most of the guys at Sil's talked. He didn't brag, or preen himself. He just told her things if she asked, and if she asked the right things, he turned on like a light. Vickie leaned her chin on her hands and looked up at him with absolutely genuine interest as he talked about...bugs. He really knew a *lot* about insects, and not just insects but birds, and deer, and snakes, and wind caves.

He volunteered out at Black Oak Park some weekends, showing people around and telling kids about the deer and the quail, the praying mantises and the poison oak. That's what he wanted to do, he said, work in the park service. He was right in the middle of an entertaining descripion of the mating habits of yellow-jackets, when he suddenly broke off, embarrassed to be talking so much, telling a girl in a bar about *bees*, but Vickie said, "No, no, go on, I'm really interested."

They were gabbing happily, heads together, when Vickie glanced up to see how Joan was getting along. She was feeling a little guilty, since Joan was getting the bad end of this deal. To her horror, Steve was trying to steer Joan over to their table. She had to act fast.

She fought down a sudden hollow feeling and tapped Phil on the wrist, where one of his ubiquitous chains lay, dull silver against the light gold hair of his arm.

"Hey Phil," she said lightly. "Let's go for a ride in that truck of yours." Knowing he was truck-proud, she was careful to include it in the wording of her invitation.

Phil looked surprised, Steve slid off the barstool, Joan threw up her hands, and Vickie's heart sank.

But Phil came through. He collected himself, grinned at her and gave her a feather-light punch on the shoulder. "Aw-wright!" They left a protesting Steve in the bar — Joan giving a thumbs-up behind his back — and walked out into the night air, holding hands.

"The motor vehicle you are about to enter," said Phil, doing a very bad Rod Serling imitation as he handed her into the truck, "is a mostly blue '56 GMC half-ton with an improved V-8 engine and a hunnert fourteen-inch bed." He slammed the door, saluted and skipped around the front of the cab. He climbed into the driver's seat and continued his rundown of specifications. "Three whitewalls, two-forty air conditioning, no AM-FM radio, and the gas gauge don't work. But," he said proudly, "Got a real nice tape deck." Which he demonstrated by filling the cab with "Whole Lotta Rosie."

"Aha, yeah, so I see," said Vickie.

"What?" yelled Phil.

Vickie leaned over and turned the music down.

Phil smiled, nodded, and turned the ignition. The improved V-8 engine drowned out the music.

Phil was in his element. He deftly steered the truck out of the parking lot, hit the street at a cool 40 MPH, screeched to the intersection and slammed the truck to a dead stop amidst squealing tires and the black smell of burning rubber.

"Where you wanna go?"

Vickie glanced out the window at the sidewalk. It seemed so much safer out there on the street. "Oh, just anywhere, I guess. As long as you get me there in one piece."

"I'll get you there in one piece, don't worry," he promised, making a solemn cross over his heart.

Vickie smiled at a bag lady standing precariously on the curb. *Am I making a big mistake?* She looked sideways at her driver, sitting easily on his specially made lambskin seatcover, with his left arm resting on the car door, his right stretched out over the steering wheel, and his head tilted forward so that his soft blond hair just touched the shoulders of his black leather vest. She snuggled back into her side of the lambskin. *Nah....*

So it was that Vickie Kirk found herself barreling out Marsh Creek Road in the cool of a summer's night in a '56 GMC half-ton with an improved V-8 and a good tape deck, driven by a metal fan who liked bugs.

From Marsh Creek Road they turned off onto a dirt road, and from the dirt road, into what Vickie could only believe was a creekbed; finally, they came to a roaring stop under an ancient live oak. Dust from the wheels wafted away, and through the branches of the oak tree you could see the stars, if you looked hard enough. Pretty good for the outskirts of a California suburb.

The truck grumbled into silence, but not the tape deck, which could keep running even when the pickup wasn't. Phil was just sitting there, tongue-tied, probably wondering if he'd made a mistake and this wasn't what she'd had in mind at all. Vickie considered conversational gambits: *Well, here we are. Sure is pretty out here at night.* Maybe, *I hope you're not one of those sexual lunatics who lures women out to secluded places in the middle of the night and forces them into performing loud — I mean lewd — and unnecessary acts.*

"Do you come here often?" she said aloud. Well, she thought she should know. She watched him mentally run through about eight different replies.

"Only in the daytime, usually," he said, glancing at her. "With bunches of little kids."

"Oh."

Vickie looked up at the tree. Phil studied the dashboard. The conversation went into suspended animation.

They lunged at each other at the same time.

Well, maybe lunged isn't exactly the right word. The slight, shy movements they made toward each other wouldn't have been taken by many people as anything but casual, but it got them where they both wanted to be: crushed together with their tongues down each other's throats.

"I'm bad! I'm nationwide!" ZZ Top screamed from the dashboard.

"Mrmpf mrmpf," said Vickie, pushing desperately at Phil. "Wait! Stop! Ygnaah!"

"What?"

"Aah, nothing. I just, you know, need some air...."

"Well, if it's *air* you want, babe," Phil laughed, "come on!" He reached over her and opened her door. "G'wan! Out!" He pushed at her until she tumbled out of the truck, and hopped out after her.

"What? What?" Vickie was a little taken aback by his sudden assertiveness. He took her hand and promenaded her to the back of the truck.

"Just step right up here," he said grandly and helped her step up to the bumper and over the tailgate.

"Wait a minute." He was back in the cab, rummaging around under the seat. "I hope it's not too dirty," he said as he vaulted expertly over the tailgate. He shook out a blanket and examined it critically.

"It'll do, I guess."

"Oh," said Vickie somewhat breathlessly, "it'll do fine."

They spread the blanket in the bed of the truck. Vickie spread herself over the blanket and Phil spread himself over Vickie. Oh my, she thought as she ran her hands under his vest, feeling the curves and hollows of his chest. Oh my.

The warm, slightly beery smell of his breath mingled with the tang coming from the leather, and Vickie just wanted to drink it all in. Phil was amenable to that. He ran his lips over her mouth and then kissed her hard, while he ever-so-gently tugged at the buttons of her shirt until he got them all undone.

"Aww, man," he said as his disappointed hands encountered a peach-colored "near-bare" designer tank top. Vickie giggled and pulled at a heavy chain hooked to his vest.

"What's this for?"

For an answer he kissed her, running his thumb over a nipple through her tank top. She wriggled under his touch, but stuck to her guns.

"No, what's it *for?*"

Phil gave her a poke. "It's not for nothing, chick. Hush up."

"Don't call me chick!" But Vickie was laughing as she struggled up off the truck bed and pulled at his hair. Her mock attack only gave him the advantage; he slid an arm around her back and yanked the tank top out of her jeans. His hands, rough, cool, calloused, cupped her bare breasts and Vickie let go of his hair and hugged him close, curling up her toes as he buried his head between her breasts.

"Mmmm...." He brought his face up to hers and licked the tip of her nose happily. Vickie smiled up at him and pulled the front of his T-shirt out of his jeans and pushed it up over his chest. They lay down, their bare skin pressed together like a secret between them.

"Uh-uhn," he said suddenly, and pushed her hands away. "You first." The words didn't quite come out with the bravado he intended and even through the darkness Vickie could tell he was blushing to his toes.

Wasn't going to stop him, though. Vickie was more than content to let him undress her, which he did with more gentleness than she would have expected from a guy wearing boots that heavy. This man liked to take his time. He didn't just pull her out of her jeans. No, he carefully unbuckled her belt, then removed her shoes, one at a time, tapping her head with the toe of one red high heel, making her wrinkle up her nose. Then he unzipped her jeans and peeled them off, a little clumsily — these things never go quite as smoothly as they do in the movies — and then he went after her stockings. All the time he was touching and kissing her, licking, biting, caressing her, nibbling at each part of her body as he uncovered it.

Finally he got down to her panties, twirled them around a finger and laughingly stuck them in his pocket. He left her the tank top, which Vickie thought was very generous of him, even though he pushed it up to get at her breasts with his hands and mouth, sending little sparks of pleasure straight up her spine and back, *zzzzzzt,* making a warm tingling between her thighs turn to a deep urgent desire that needed satisfying.

Vickie hadn't been this excited since she let her first date feel her up when she was fifteen. Phil grinned his lopsided grin and moved up onto her and she wrapped her legs around him, reveling in the coarse feel of his jeans rubbing against her crotch, the smooth leather against her breasts, the feel of his cock hard under the denim.

"Look at the stars," he said, and kissed her neck, her breasts,, her stomach, not missing any of her if he could help it. Vickie didn't think the stars were all that interesting. She opened her eyes and watched his blond head going down on her. His tongue slid right down there and Vickie came to her senses and sat bolt upright. She startled her new lover halfway out the back end of the truck.

"Phil!" she wailed. "What if somebody *comes?*"

"*Nobody's* gonna fucking come if you keep jumping around like that."

"I mean what if somebody comes *here?*"

"Nobody's gonna come up here," Phil declared. He jerked his thumb at his chest. "I own the place."

"Oh, you do not."

"Sure I do. I claim squatter's rights." He gave her a little shove. "Chick, you worry too much. Are you gonna lay back and take it or am I gonna hafta *tie* you to this truck?"

"Oh...." Vickie sank back down on the blanket.

Pleased at his successful domination of a willing woman, Phil took right up where he'd left off. His head went down between her legs and he reached up and spread his hands over both her breasts.

Vickie closed her eyes and was floating above them; she could see them like that, she naked and spread in the back end of an old truck, Phil in his jeans and boots and leather...her pleasure took a sharp turn and she was going 'round the bend at ninety miles an hour, and then she was all but climbing out of the truck bed. Phil was getting a bumpy ride.

She rolled over on her stomach and buried her face in her arm, embarrassed as she always was after coming like that. Phil clambered up and rolled her on her back again. She squinted up at him with one eye.

"Have we met?"

Phil kissed her. "Silly chick."

He shrugged off his vest and pulled his shirt over his head.

Vickie reached out as he unbuckled his belt. "Lemme help."

"Aw, you're in no shape to help anyone." But he slid his hip over close to her upturned face and gave her a smug, wicked little smile as he pulled the zipper down and wiggled free of his jeans. He was wearing yellow bikini jockey shorts.

Vickie was delighted. "Aren't you afraid to go out in public with those on? I mean you might get in an accident and have to go to the hospital!"

Phil dropped a boot on the metal truck bed, making an alarming clunk. He threw a sock at her.

"Yecch." Holding the sock gingerly by thumb and forefinger, she flung it over the side of the truck.

Divested of all his masculine finery, Phil became shy. He seemed so much more vulnerable now, and of course, he was, since Vickie made a grab for his cock as soon as she realized he was lapsing into one of his awkward silences. He looked so pale and smooth in the moonlight, like a teenager, his chest hairless and glowing white. His muscular shoulders and arms made her sigh, and his behind was soft and covered with tiny hairs that delighted her fingers as she guided him to her.

Not that he needed any guidance. After his initial attack of shyness he was all over her and, furthermore, rather pushy.

"Wait," she panted. "Wait."

He looked down at her in disbelief. "What do you *mean*, wait, chick?"

"Don't call me a — whoops! Aha...yikes, there you go."

"Wait...hell...."

He started out slow, leaning over her so that his hair tickled her nose, but now Vickie was getting pretty pushy herself. She ran her hands down his back and pulled him down on her, arching her back to meet him halfway as he thrust faster and deeper and harder, buried her face in his shoulder moaning, desperate, clawing, crying out; she was going down that hill at ninety miles an hour and Phil had the throttle all the way out.

"Oh, God, I'm gonna come!"

"Do...multiplication tables," she panted. "It's supposed...to help."

He gave her one astonished look, then clapped his hand over her mouth to stifle any more advice. She felt him go all rigid and then he was thrusting again, but slower now and without rhythm, and then all the air seemed to go out of him in a whoosh and he slumped on top of her.

"Mrmpf mrmpf." She got her mouth open wide enough to bite one of his fingers.

"Oh, sorry." He rolled off, but snuggled up against her, and for a long time they lay listening to each other breathe. Vickie was thinking: "I hope he has a box of Kleenex or something." Gradually the world came back into focus: the gnarled old oak tree, the sound of nightbirds, the stars, the slender half-moon, the hard bed of the truck under her tailbone, the radio.

"Iddly iddly iddly!" screamed something up front in the cab. "Keerrang keerrang keerraaaannng!"

Phil ran a finger lightly along her throat. "Look at the stars," he said softly. Vickie tilted her head back and he put his mouth on the base of her throat and blew a loud razzberry.

That must have been what started them off again. You can never tell about some people.

The stars had started to flicker out when, all cleaned up and dressed, they piled back into the front of the truck. Phil changed the tape to something loud, and drowned it out by starting the engine. They bumped and bounced back to civilization. When they reached the edge of Marsh Creek Road, Phil slowed the truck with unusual gentleness and sat for a minute with both arms stretched over the steering wheel, looking at something beyond the windshield.

"You know, Vickie...." He hesitated.

She waited. Not chick. Vickie.

He turned and smiled a little lopsidedly and punched her lightly on the shoulder. "I like you."

Then he hit the gas and the truck careened onto the asphalt, kicking up a mess of dust and one hell of a noise.

Vickie laughed and leaned out the window to catch the night wind on her face. "Awww*right!*"

Shaman's Eyes

Nancy Blackett

The drums would not begin until just before sunset, but I woke with my heart pounding like twenty drums. Before I opened my eyes I knew today was the day of the maiden's dance, and in my mind, I pictured the boy of my choice. He was slim, with that wiry strength that seems to come as much from nerve as from muscle. I had noticed him at hunts and dances, and we had often talked. He had a warrior's courage combined with the inward-seeing eyes of a shaman, a mixture I had never seen before, yet he did not seem at war with himself; only guarded, though we talked easily together once we started. It was not his guardedness I loved, but what it protected.

Did he love me? I did not know. But in the maiden's dance, it was the girls who chose, and those choices, more often than not, led to marriage. My real worry today was not whether he loved me, for if I entered his hut, we would lie together, however he felt. My fear was that some other girl wanted him also and that the dance would carry her to his hut before me. My chances were good though, for many girls would not want a stranger. He was not from our village, or even of our people. His own village had been destroyed by white men, and he had come to live with us a few summers before. But he was not strange to me. He had learned our ways, and we could talk together about little things.

I heard my mother moving about the teepee and put away my fears. I had much to do. My teepee was ready, made of eleven buffalo skins that my father had hunted. I went over my dress once more to make sure every bead and fringe was in place and securely sewn. As I was washing my hair, a new worry entered my mind. What if I entered the wrong hut by mistake? I had never heard of it happening, but what if...? When my hair was dry, I ran to look at the huts again. Of course I would know his. I had watched him build it, knew every stick of it.

Mother called me to eat, though I had no desire for food. The day stretched on forever. Then, suddenly, the drums began. I took my place in the line, taking the hands of the girls on either side of me. They were from my village; I had touched their hands countless times as we played and worked together, yet now I felt a tingle of fear at their touch. It was as if they were strangers, though we would be friends again when this night was over as surely as the sun would rise in the morning.

We danced the pattern we had learned, and as the beat changed, we danced toward the circle of huts and began to go around it. My eyes sought his hut — ah! The door covering was not dropped, and I was coming closer, closer, and no one broke the line. Now I was in front of it, and I released the hands of my dear friends, and stooped to enter the hut.

He sat, wrapped in a buffalo robe, looking like a chief but too young, his face more guarded than I had ever seen it. My heart sank. He had hoped for another, and he was trying not to show his disappointment. I said his name in my mind, "Ladan, Ladan!" for neither of us would speak aloud that night. I prayed that lying with him, I could change his mind. It sometimes happened; I had heard women speak of it. I brushed his cheek with my hand. He was so soft and young. Perhaps it was only that. Brave warriors were not always fearless with women. I opened his robe slowly, looked at his naked body and gasped.

Where something should be, there was nothing. For the briefest moment, I wondered if he had met with some horrible mishap in the hunt, or in war, or in the raid that had killed his people. In the next instant, I realized that nothing was missing, everything was there. But Ladan was a girl. And afraid. It was this secret she guarded. The boys in her village must have known, and her strength and courage would have won their silence. No one in my village knew, or had said.

And what now? I had desired Ladan so long, and here we were, and I felt only confusion. She reached out and laid her palm not on my breast, but on my breastbone. I felt the bone melt and open under her hand. She was a shaman. I laid my palm on her breastbone, felt the rapid beat of her heart, and felt desire blossom in me like fire, like running water. The fear left her face, and the bravery as well, and the strength, and the inward look, and all I saw was softness. I knew that it was desire and that she saw the same in me. We smiled and her hand moved to my breast. My hand moved at the same moment, in a dance no one had taught us. She spread out her robe and I took off my dress and we lay together on the robe, touching, stroking, watching the happiness in each other's faces until it grew too dark to see. The hut smelled of earth and leaves, of the wild, not of the village. We only became aware of the drumming when it stopped.

We did not speak, but her fingers were counting mine, were drawing an outline of my body, telling me how smooth and round my buttocks were, singing to me of the softness and strength between my legs. It felt so good to me that I had to touch her too, and tell her in the same way how intricate her ears were, how many times I could stroke her belly without ever tiring of it, and how her shaman's eyes had haunted all my days and dreams. When her pleasure grew so intense that she must cry out of it, she began to weep, and I know that she did not weep from disappointment, but from relief that her loneliness was over.

Nor was I ever disappointed in her, for she was as good a hunter as any man in the village, and, later, there were enough children left motherless from the white man's raids that I never did miss birthing one of my own.

Just a Bad Day

Lisa Wright

Sara stabbed her key into the lock and jiggled it around. "This is all I need," she muttered under her breath. "Damn key never works right. What a lousy day."

First there had been the coffee she spilled on her new skirt, then came the fight with her boss. To top it all off, some jerk from Vermont, of all places, had parked his van in her space. She had had to park two blocks away and run home through a drenching rain.

Sara hooked her dripping hair behind her ear and struggled more vigorously with the key. Finally, it clicked into place. Visions of a hot shower and a warm bed soothed her until she stepped inside. An unfamiliar suitcase sat on the floor by her roommate's door. "Kathy?" Sara called. "I thought you were working tonight."

"She is," a male voice answered from the kitchen. Sara grabbed for the doorknob, ready to bolt.

A man emerged, drying his hands on a dish towel. He has to be Kathy's brother, Sara realized. He looks just like her.

"You must be Sara," he said, smiling. "I'd know you

anywhere. Kathy talks about you all the time." He extended his hand. "I'm Matt, Kathy's brother."

Matt, she thought. He's the potter from Vermont. Vermont! That's got to be his van. What the hell is he doing here?

Sara hadn't moved since she first heard his voice. Her hand still held the doorknob and a puddle was forming on the rug beneath her. She glared at this intruder half in anger, half in amazement.

Matt dropped his hand back to his side, and shifted his weight from one foot to the other. "Look," he said, "I'm sorry to intrude with no notice. I got a call last night that a space had opened up in the craft show here this weekend. I've been trying to get into this show for years, and I couldn't pass it up."

Come on, Sara, she told herself, straighten up! This is Kathy's brother, not Jack the Ripper. She let go of the doorknob and forced herself to smile. "I'm sorry," she said. "Of course you're welcome to stay."

He looked relieved.

"You'll have to forgive me. I've had a bad day."

"I can see that!" he laughed.

"Make yourself at home while I get out of these wet clothes."

The hot water poured over her body, melting the tension in her shoulders, rounding the sharp edges of her annoyance. He really is rather attractive, Sara decided. The square jaw and wide mouth looked much better on Matt than on Kathy. She remembered a photo that Kathy had shown her of Matt, shirtless. Very nice, she decided. Very nice.

Sara began lathering herself absentmindedly. No one could be as wonderful as Kathy says Matt is, she told herself. Warm, sensitive, thoughtful. Yeah, but taking my parking space was not exactly thoughtful. Still, there is something about him.

The smooth, slippery movements of her hands felt luscious on her belly, her thighs. She made lazy circles around her breasts, squeezing the nipples gently between her fingers. One soapy hand glided down to her pubes. Her fingers slid over and between her labia. A tingling warmth spread into her abdomen and her inner thighs.

Sara reached up and removed the hand-held shower head from the wall. She switched the setting from spray to a pulsating jet and aimed it at her groin.

A blast of icy cold water hit her clitoris. "Shit!" she screamed, and slammed off the water, gasping for breath.

There was a timid knock at the door. "Are you okay?" Matt asked.

"I ran out of hot water rather suddenly," Sara growled.

"I guess that was my fault," he admitted through the door. "I turned the dishwasher on and forgot you were in the shower. Sorry!"

Sara shook her head and sighed. "This is not my day." She turned the water back on just long enough to finish rinsing off.

Half an hour later, Sara emerged from her room, dry and dressed in jeans and her favorite sweater. A delicious aroma hung in the air. Her mouth began to water as she crossed the living room. "Something sure smells good," she called.

She rounded the corner into the kitchen and gasped. Matt looked up from where he was kneeling in front of the oven and grinned. "I thought you could use a nice dinner," he said.

"Nice? I think I'm in love!"

The table was covered with a clean tablecloth. A salad, a bottle of white wine and two wine glasses were set out.

"Pour yourself some wine," said Matt, closing the oven door. "Dinner will be ready in a few minutes."

He finished setting the table while Sara sipped her wine. He seemed totally at ease. She had never known a man who was so at home in the kitchen.

"Not all men are helpless," Matt said, reading her mind. "I've lived alone for six years. It was either learn how to cook and clean or live in a pigsty and eat Burger King. It didn't take me long to decide."

Sara laughed. The wine felt warm inside her. She felt a familiar tingle of excitement in the nape of her neck. "I've been a real bitch ever since I came home," she said. "Do you think we could start all over again?"

"Sounds good to me," Matt agreed. He walked the short distance to Sara's chair and extended his hand. "Hello," he said. "You must be Sara. I'm Matt, Kathy's brother."

They shook hands.

Dinner was superb. Chicken stuffed with peaches and mushrooms was accompanied by tender, young asparagus and hot, crusty bread.

"I wish I could cook like that," Sara said as she pushed aside her empty plate.

"You could if you wanted to," said Matt. "Kathy tells me you're pretty talented too."

"Talented? Me? What do you mean?"

"Kathy showed me the sweater you made for her. It's beautiful."

Sara blushed. "No, it was just...."

"Just beautiful," he insisted. His eyes never left her face. She blushed as she felt his gaze. "Did you knit the one you're wearing?" Sara nodded, feeling him drink her in. She couldn't take her eyes off him. It was hard to breathe. This is crazy, she thought, I hardly know this man.

Matt reached over and ran his hand along her sleeve. "Cotton, isn't it?"

Again she nodded. She watched him caress her arm. His touch was electric. Her gaze moved from his hand to his face. He was looking at her.

"I feel like I know so much about you already," he said softly.

Sara didn't trust her voice. An ache of longing filled her lap.

"The dishes," she said, her voice cracking. She cleared her throat and tried again,

"I'd better do the dishes now."

Matt let go of her arm, reluctantly, and smiled. "I'll dry."

Sara snatched up the plates and carried them to the sink. This is moving much too fast, she thought. I've got to get hold of myself.

The sink filled with hot, soapy water. She plunged her hands in and tried to concentrate on the dishes. Almost immediately her hair fell into her eyes. "Damn it," she said, blowing at the hair. She tried flipping it back with a toss of her head, but it was no use.

"Here, let me help," Matt said. He came up close behind her. Gently, he gathered her hair together and drew it back, letting his hands glide against her face. "Your hair is so soft," he whispered into her neck.

Sara's knees went weak. She was breathing in short gasps. Every inch of her body tingled.

He kissed her delicately behind her ear lobe. "Sara...," he said. Her body was alive with his touch. He kissed her again, moving down her neck to the curve of her shoulder. He held her hair and encircled her waist, drawing her body against his. She gripped the sink with soapy hands. Matt reached for a dish towel and gently wiped her hands dry.

His mouth opened on the curve of her neck, licking, sucking. She pressed back against his body, feeling his hardness against her ass. Sara reached back with one hand and stroked his leg, kneading his thigh with her finger. "Oh God....," she whimpered, "I want you." Her cunt ached, soaking her jeans.

Matt turned her around. His eyes searched hers. Then their mouths were together, wet and hungry. His hands slid up under her sweater, over her back, running down her side, grazing the edge of her breasts. His touch sent shocks through her body. His hands found her breasts, fondling them, teasing the hard nipples. One hand slipped down inside her pants as Sara fumbled with his belt, his button, his zipper. His cock flew out as she tugged his jeans down. It was hard and smooth. She lowered herself to her knees and took his cock in both hands. She licked a pearly drop of cum off the tip and then slid the smooth stalk into her mouth...once, twice.

"Wait, wait," he moaned. He slipped out of her mouth and kneeled down, facing her. His hand slid down through her pubic hair and inside. Her cunt exploded. He drew out his fingers and smeared the cum on her breasts, licking it off as his hand returned to her vagina.

They struggled out of their jeans, kicking them aside. "Come inside me. Please, now!" Sara begged. Matt moved between her thighs and rubbed his cock against her clit until she came again. Then he stretched deep inside as her cunt contracted. She gripped his arms, and he plunged deeper and deeper inside her.

Hello!" Kathy's voice called from the living room. "I'm home. Is anyone here?"

Rapid Transit

Mickey Warnock

The subway train rolled out of the Lafayette station about eight thirty on Sunday night. Linda and I were alone in the last car, on our way home from dinner at her mother's house.

I looked across at Linda, who stared out the window next to her. She was going to get it when we got home. All day long she had teased me sexually when her mother wasn't watching. She had a habit of doing that to me in public, confessing that she enjoyed it, because she knew I'd ravage her when we got home.

Halfway to the Orinda station, the train screeched to a halt. I sighed deeply, leaning back. Just what I needed, a delay.

"Shit, what is it this time?" I groaned, when after five minutes the train hadn't budged.

"Hang tight, babe, it's probably another train ahead of us," said Linda.

"ATTENTION PASSENGERS. DUE TO MECHANICAL DIFFICULTIES OF THE TRAIN AHEAD OF US, WE WILL BE DELAYED UNTIL FURTHER NOTICE. WE APOLOGIZE FOR THIS INCONVENIENCE."

"Damn," I muttered, and lit a cigarette.

"Wanna play cards, Mick?"

"Very funny, Lin. I just want to get home!"

"What's the hurry, we don't have to work tomorrow," she said, reaching over to pat my leg.

"I know, but you were pretty bad today when your mom wasn't looking." I took a drag of my cigarette.

"Oh, poor thing, is Mickey all hot and bothered?"

I closed my eyes and pretended to ignore her. At that moment, Linda jumped up, straddling my lap. I didn't move. She took my head in her hands, breathing warmly in my ear. I shuddered.

"Mickey, I want you...now," she whispered.

I opened my eyes, realizing what she had just said.

"On a subway train?"

"Why not?" she said, lightly kissing me.

"What if someone...." I tried to say, but Linda's lips covered mine.

She started to unbutton my shirt, and I fumbled with hers. We pulled them open in unison, embracing, our warm bare breasts pressed together. Linda's lips left mine. Her tongue slid down my neck to my bare shoulder, which she lightly nibbled. Just then, the train began to move.

"Watch out," I laughed, grabbing onto Linda, who almost fell backwards. She began to do up her shirt when I grabbed her hands. "Not so fast. I want you to fuck me before we get back to Oakland!" I was quite serious. I couldn't wait any longer, not after this.

Shaking her head, Linda undid my fly, and I hers. I gave a low moan as her hand slid between my legs, slipping a couple of fingers inside me. I eased my right hand down her pants. We stroked each other as the train rolled into Orinda. I slightly opened my eyes over Linda's shoulder when the doors parted, expecting some poor soul to walk in. No one did.

Linda curled over me so that I could slip another finger inside her, and my free hand grabbed her dangling breast. The train roared through the tunnels. Linda shoved all her fingers in, and I winced. She was fucking me quickly, roughly. Her teeth dug into my neck, and the rest of my hand squeezed into her cunt.

"Oh, Jesus!" I cried out at Rockridge station, coming in a flood into Linda's hand.

Her hand slowed, but mine moved quicker. She pumped it,

racing, panting in my ear, "I'm coming, I'm coming," releasing me as she gave a long, low moan.

We held each other quietly, catching our breath.

"Better get dressed, babe, we're almost home," I whispered. We limped out of our empty car at the Oakland station...and two other dykes walked on.

Visit to The Mighoren

Emily Alward

What have I gotten myself into? Angelica thought. A wave of panic jolted her.

The Moonmist was crowded. Hundreds of candlepoints flickered in chandeliers, soft light reflecting off crackleglass windows and the women's dresses. Subdued conversation swirled around her. A single strand of melody, the pure notes of a lyre, threaded beneath the babble. The scene resembled one of the elegant bistros in Angelica's hometown, the ancient city of Toronto.

Except...the men were all exraordinarily attractive. She'd noted it before, the predominance of male good looks on this planet. Her new colleague Rihanna had just smiled and said, "Of course, Angie, selection pressures."

She shot a worried look at Rihanna now. The Cobalean woman was surveying the room with an anticipatory air.

"What do I do?" Angelica whispered.

"Well, just pick one you like and go talk to him," her friend said. Apparently Rihanna herself was engrossed in the first part of this process. Her gaze darted between a nearby archway and a table across the room. A dark man with a gaze of smouldering intensity sat at one end, a cheerfully insouciant blond at the other.

My god, I have all these choices too, Angelica realized. She began to tingle inside, a wholly unexpected feeling. Still, she was scared. "But what if the man doesn't like...." she protested.

"Silly girl! Just go on, don't waste our money."

Rihanna gave her a gentle shove. Angelica stumbled away from the entrance foyer. She walked slowly between rows of tables, a glaze of unreality fogging her mind. This couldn't be happening to her, a well-brought-up young Terran woman who'd come here to study antique texts.

"Good evening, *nemelyya*."

She looked into eyes as blue as the Cobalean clouds.

"Good evening," she managed to murmur. She pulled out a chair and sank into it. She had serious doubt that her feet — or her courage — would carry her any farther. "My name is Angelica," she added shakily, unable to think of any brighter way to open a conversation.

"Damik mir Nymet," he replied. "Would you like some wine while you look around?"

"Yes, please. Some for yourself, too," she added, remembering good manners. She stared discreetly at her new acquaintance while he signaled a server. Those incredible azure eyes were set in an equally glorious face. It reminded her of those on the prehistoric Greek statues, or some character — was it Redford? Voight? — in the old 2-D dramas. He was somewhat taller than herself, nicely muscled — she searched her memory for the Cobalean word. *Gherique* — yes, that was it. Would he be *zacuir* too? She blushed furiously as the question invaded her thoughts. Her mentors had urged rapid acculturation. She was sure they didn't have this in mind. Her cheeks continued to sting, and she looked down in confusion. The outer robe Rihanna had loaned her had come unfastened. She didn't know what etiquette required here, so she left it open.

Damik held out a goblet of bubbly pink wine to her. He raised his own in salutation. "To the *nemelyya's* health."

Angelica gave a gracious nod. Talk to him, Rihanna had told her. Whatever could she say? She'd never known it was possible to feel at the same time so awkward and so aroused. She stole another glance across the table. He sat there with one sturdy hand cupped around the goblet, regarding her. Confidence was written all over his face. Somehow she'd have felt calmer if he'd shown some hint of uncertainty too.

"Mir Nymet. Isn't that an archonial name?" she finally asked.

"*Hai*, it is."

He was polite, even courtly, but was obviously waiting for her to take the conversational initiative. Am I expected to take the initiative in other things too?, she wondered. Panic touched her again.

"But...you're from one of the sixty families." The sixty archonial families formed the pinnacle of Cobalean social structure. "However did you end up in a place like this?"

"Oh." He laughed, but looked shocked, too, at her question. "You're not from this planet at all, are you?"

Angelica shook her head. She was relieved to find herself capable of conversation, but in all fairness she should tell him the rest. "I'm from off- planet. A visiting student at the Institute. So if you don't want anything to do with me, it's all right — "

"*Nyai*. You're a very alluring woman, off-planet or no. I'd be delighted to service you, but if you choose someone else, I won't be offended."

Angelica squirmed. An anticipatory quiver shot through her labia at the overt suggestion. Damn, he was attractive. Luckily this place was not as she had pictured it, with the men half-clothed. She would be attacking him, making a complete fool of herself....

"Mind if we just talk for a little while?" She struggled to sound collected. Reaching for her social scientist facade, she said, "I'd like to ask you some questions."

"Go ahead." He was still looking at her, steadily and appreciatively. Did she imagine a hint of amusement at her discomfort?

"Why are you — I mean, have you fallen into disgrace or anything? I thought the archonial families were very proud."

"So we are." Yes, he definitely sounded amused. "No, I'm not in disgrace, merely waiting for a suitable marriage to be arranged."

"And they let you work here in the meantime?" None of her ideas about the *mighoren* were proving true. She'd supposed it would be staffed by desperate men in some sort of indentured status, like geishas in the old Japanese tales. Instead, this Damik claimed to belong to the ruling class of the planet. He wore the self-assurance shown by aristocrats anywhere in the galaxy. She studied him openly this time, and began to tingle again. Suddenly she wanted very much to try him.

"Do I get a reference in your report as a source?" he asked.

Surprise warred with desire in Angelica. So he was familiar with the apparatus of scholarship, too. An entirely suitable man. Would she be brave enough to carry this through? "If you wish," she murmured. "Please tell me how it works."

"*Hai,* I come here once a week. It provides pocket cash, enjoyable female company, and..." he shrugged, "recommendations from a good *mighoren* increase one's value as a potential husband."

"Oh." She would never understand Cobalean society; it was too strange. The whole planet was floating in sensuality. That didn't matter, though, at this moment. She felt a part of it; she wanted to feel his arms around her, to welcome him into her body. Angelica reached out her hand to Damik. "I'm not looking any further."

The sense of unreality hit her again. How had she ever gotten into this situation? A collage of recent happenings swirled through her head. It had all started a week ago, with another glass of wine....

Shards from a goblet fell at Angelica's feet. The pink wine ebbed around the shattered pieces.

"Dammit," she muttered, fortunately in her native Terran dialect. The spill was an incredible gaffe for a representative of Empire culture to make.

"Your pardon, *nemelyya,*" she said quickly in her shaky Cobalean.

"Never worry, my dear. A server will clean it up," the other replied kindly. "You were saying, about the ancient books?"

"*Hai.*" Angelica fell into the alien language's forms. "I agree with your philosophers' conclusions that they originated off-planet. How they came to be on Cobale is a puzzle."

The woman asked more questions, which Angelica answered as best she could. She was quite nervous now. The official was all graciousness, but she kept staring speculatively at Angelica, almost as if the young Terran scholar had some pitiable condition evident to everyone but herself.

Later, as the reception began to break up, her new colleagues came by, and offered to walk her back to the Institute dormitory.

Angelica was relieved and grateful at the gesture. She'd only known Rihanna and Josinne a few short weeks, but they were the only friends she had on the whole planet. Both were merry and easy to talk to. Perhaps they could tell her if she'd made some irreparable social blunder.

Once out in the capital's narrow streets, the cool air revived her. She listened idly to Josinne's chatter about various men she'd talked to at the party. Just like a teen-ager on any world, Angelica reflected. Well, not quite. Josinne's talk was peppered with terms that weren't in Angelica's hastily-acquired Cobalean vocabulary. I will have to look them up, she thought. What does *zacuir* mean? What is *gherique*?

"And did you have a good time, Angelica?" Rihanna asked.

"Um, mostly. Except for my stupidity in breaking that goblet."

Rihanna patted her shoulder sympathetically. "I'm sure everyone understands."

"I'm not so sure," Angelica muttered. "That official kept staring at me like I was a freak."

"Not a freak, Angie. It's perfectly obvious that you're in need."

"In need of what?" Angelica blurted out. She wasn't sure she understood the implication. Insofar as she did, it was highly insulting, at least to a woman of Terran origin. She reminded herself about cultural relativity. "It's just culture shock," she said aloud.

"Culture shock?" In the two moons' glow, she could see the incredulous look the Cobalean women exchanged. Then they burst out laughing.

"Tell me, friend. Is it Terran custom to spill wine on a high official of state?" Rihanna teased.

"Of course not." Angelica sulked. The conversation was taking an uncomfortable turn.

"How long is it since you've had a lover?" Rihanna asked. Her voice was very soft, and without malice.

"Eight months," Angelica said through clenched teeth. Actually, it had been a year and eight months. These women had no right to ask, of course. Personal relationships were just that — personal — and one didn't enter them without a deep commitment. Geoffrey's commitment had suddenly dissolved when she had decided to study xenolinguistics. The memory still hurt.

"Poor girl," Rihanna said. Angelica snapped out of her reverie. The massive gates of the Institute grounds loomed ahead. She was eager to run up to her room and escape into her studies. She politely thanked Rihanna and Josinne for their concern. Despite the gaps in understanding, she would after all be working with them for the next few months.

"That's all right," Josinne said. She added lightly, "Now we know what we'll give you for your birthday next week."

The days spun by. Angelica immersed herself in research. Books from the Institute library piled up in her room. She sat now, warmed by a beam of the blue smoky sunlight, punching inquiries into her keyboard. She was trying to identify the terms Josinne had used a few evenings ago.

ZAQUIR? she queried.

ZAQUIR appeared on the screen, followed immediately by NETE, which meant "no exact Terran equivalent"; a common notation in alien language study.

The definition appeared. ZAQUIR: 2310 AD: STRONG, VIRILE. Okay, clear enough.

Then another notation jumped up. ZACUIR: 2339 AD: CAPABLE OF EXCELLENT PROLONGED THRUSTING; CAPABLE OF BRINGING A WOMAN TO A CONTINUOUS ORGASMIC PLATEAU.

Wow, Angelica thought, her neochristian upbringing surfacing for a moment. What a hell of a thing for a young girl like Josinne to be talking about openly.

Then her professional curiosity took over. Here was an interesting insight into Cobalean culture. Societies developed terms for those distinctions important to them. She'd vaguely suspected that women's sexual enjoyment was rated higher on Cobale than in the worlds of the Terran Empire. Here was proof. Terran Standard had dozens of scientific and vulgar words for sex. But none of them precisely defined anything about a man's talents for bringing pleasure to a woman.

She punched in another word. GHERIQUE? Again, NETE. Then, GHERIQUE: WELL- FORMED; OF GOOD PHYSIQUE. And, TERM INDICATES A MALE BODY WHICH IS WELL-TONED BUT NOT MUSCLE-BOUND. MILD MESOMORPH TYPE; FIRM ARMS AND BUTTOCKS; ADEQUATELY LARGE PENIS.

Angelica wondered, do these women think of men only as sex objects? She tried a third word.

AGIDAL? AGIDAL: COURTEOUS; WELL-MANNERED. COMPETENT.

Then another note flickered in, preceded by the "!" which indicated disagreement with previous definitions. AGIDAL IS IMPOSSIBLE TO DEFINE SIMPLY. IT IS THE MALE COROLLARY TO THE PRIME VIRTUE WHICH ARCHONIAL FEMALES ARE EXPECTED TO EXEMPLIFY. INCLUDES CONNOTATIONS OF GOOD BREEDING, COURAGE, INTELLIGENCE, PHYSICAL PROWESS, CONFIDENCE, CONGENIALITY, COMPASSION. OFTEN USED WITH ALIREL (C.F. APPRECIATIVE AFFECTION AND LOYALTY TOWARD ONE'S LADY) TO DESCRIBE THE IDEAL MAN. Enough of this, Angelica told herself. She should be coding the crumbling texts she had been sent here to study, not brooding over Cobalean sexuality.

The doorchimes jangled. Angelica leapt up guiltily to answer. Rihanna and Josinne stood in the entrance. Both of them beamed at her.

"We have a surprise for you," Rihanna said happily.

Josinne leaned over and placed a light kiss on Angelica's cheek. "Happy birthday, Angelica. Enjoy your gift." She shifted her books and hurried down the hall, obviously on her way to some seminar.

Rihanna followed Angelica back into the room. The Cobalean woman's eyes danced with delight.

"So what's the big surprise?" Angelica asked.

"Oh, Angie, I do hope you like it," Rihanna said. "You are going to the *mighoren* tonight, and I am going with you."

Angelica was quiet for a moment, trying to identify the unfamiliar term. She knew the root word. *Mighir* was the estrus period Cobalean females experienced once a month. From the shimmer surrounding her, Rihanna appeared to be well into *mighir* now.

"Excuse me a minute," Angelica said. She walked over and keyed the new word into her computer. The definition leapt onto the screen. She frowned.

"Let's make sure I understand you," Angelica said. Shock battled with concern over her friend's feelings. She phrased her question carefully.

"Are you saying you're taking me...to...a place...where I pay for...men...to have sex with me?"

"Why yes, I suppose that's the Terran interpretation," Rihanna said matter-of-factly. "Except that you don't have to pay tonight, Angie. Josinne and I are treating you."

Angelica sighed. It was completely unthinkable, of course.

Yet Rihanna stood there wriggling with enthusiasm, awaiting her thanks. She'd have to explain her refusal diplomatically. Then a twinge of mischievous curiosity hit her, asking, why *not* just agree and see what it's like? She pushed the thought away.

"Look, Rihanna, it's very kind of you, but I just can't accept. I'd find it too...degrading."

"There's nothing degrading about it!" The other woman flared. "The Moonmist has only high-class men. Josinne goes there every month; she's from one of the most distinguished families on Cobale, and her mother includes *mighoren*-fees in her allowance so she won't go into delirium. Or do something disgraceful. Besides, I went to all the trouble to get reservations, and even the synthetic *mighir*-cream for you — that's almost contraband...." Rihanna sank into a chair and started crying.

Angelica had never expected tears. She was as unnerved as when she'd read the definition. Her pre-embarkation briefing continually emphasized the dangers culture gaps posed to the naive, and the responsibility of the visiting scholar to bridge them. She fidgeted uncertainly. Finally she gathered her composure and reached over to clasp Rihanna's hand, as she'd seen Cobalean women do so often for reassurance. "I'd go, if I could be sure I wouldn't be too uncomfortable," she said.

Rihanna wiped the tears away.

"You won't be. Once you're there, you'll be so excited."

Angelica looked at her dubiously.

"Think about it this way," Rihanna said. She'd resumed her normal rational tone. "If I were a guest scholar on Terra, you'd want to entertain me, wouldn't you? Maybe take me to a 'nightclub' or a concert? Well, this is no different. Except it's more necessary — and more fun." A blissful smile touched her face.

"All right," Angelica conceded. "Just tell me what I need to know and do."

"Nature will take care of that," Rihanna giggled.

"But what do I wear? What if the man can't perform on demand?"

"Wear whatever you like." Rihanna apparently thought the second question too ridiculous to answer. "I'll come by for you at sunfall. All right?"

"All right," Angelica said uneasily.

Shaking free from her memories, Angelica examined the room Damik had led her to. There was no bed, Angelica noticed instantly. One corner held a *conneghe,* the plush-covered area with varying slopes she had seen defined as a "conversation-pit." Now she doubted such a definition. She imagined herself spread out against it, Damik thrusting into her — if she ever figured out how to get to that stage. Angelica was no innocent, but she'd never been in a situation where she'd been expected to take the lead. Certainly not one in which her own wishes took precedence. Just how did one proceed?

Her face felt flushed again. An independent will seized her hands. They wanted to reach out, caress his arms and shoulders, trace slowly down his chest. No. What they really wanted was to tear off his clothes and reach for his penis, tantalizing him, then guiding it slowly, blissfully, into her.

She wasn't sure it could happen, with the difference in biological programming. She glanced down at her arms. The cream had not worn off. Her skin glittered in the lamplight, and she caught a whiff of the unfamiliar musky scent. Rihanna had assured her that the cream worked as well as the real pheromones. She hoped so. It would be unbearable, to be so in need — worse, to have it show, and then find the man unwilling or unable to meet her expectations.

Damik walked to a door opposite and drew some curtains back. "There's a grotto garden and pool. We can have a swim first, or order dinner, if you prefer. Most women don't," he added in an offhand tone.

Angelica took a deep breath. Silhouetted against the amethyst night sky, the planes of his face and body stunned her. He was even more delicious than she'd thought. She had to do something.

"No, we can swim later," she said. "What do I do?"

"It's customary to remove the *medora* first. In fact, it's essential." He smiled gently. Amusement twinkled in his blue eyes, but it was benign. He's enjoying this more than I am, she realized with surprise.

He peeled off his robe. She was trembling.

"*Hai?*" She whispered the all-purpose Cobalean word that could mean "well..." or "maybe..." or "yes."

Suddenly Damik was beside her, turning her around and pulling her against him. Their lips met in one lingering kiss, then the clothes came off. Angelica wasn't quite sure of the sequence, her own body's urgent seeking was too intense, but she knew she was flinging aside his jacket, shirt and trousers with unseemly speed. She nestled against him, her nipples erect and brushing over his magnificent chest. Somehow they ended up in the *conneghe*. A slightly-slanting surface met her back. She felt its soft, resilient support and they paused for a half-moment, savoring their shared desire.

His hands cupped each side of her body just below her waist. The touch aroused her beyond all belief. She pushed up to him. For a torturous moment she sought in vain. She would be suspended forever, she feared, his phallus beckoning like a lodestar. Then he was within her. She moaned with pleasure, and heard Damik murmuring the Cobalean love-word, *"Ticara, ticara...."*

They made love for a long, long time. Angelica had never been so satisfactorily pleasured before. She rode through waves of ecstasy, each crest taking her a little higher, till perception shattered in a storm of stars.

In the tranquil afterwash, her fingers wandered tenderly over his body and she reached for an endearment too. *"Tiru...."*

But that was not the end. Much to Angelica's surprise, when she roused herself to thank and dismiss him, Damik demurred. There was no time limit, he said, and didn't she want to enjoy some of the other features of the *mighoren*?

They swam in the grotto garden's pool, lit by opalescent nightmist. They ordered a small supper. Her tension dissipated by what they'd shared, Angelica discovered normal conversational skills returning. Or more than normal. She found the stories he told genuinely interesting, and not only for their insights into Cobalean culture. For his part, Damik asked question after question about her past life, and beamed approval when she explained how hard she'd worked for the chance to go off-planet.

Angelica recalled, seemingly at random, that the Cobalean word for marriage applied only to certain formal arrangements within the upper class. For all other attachments, the word "bond" was used. A comfortable rapport flowed between her and this man now, a sharing she'd never forget. Well, she thought, we've created some sort of a bond, however tenuous.

"Damik," she said. She hesitated, munching on a succulent river clam while summoning her next sentence. "You're a really good person. I don't know what I expected when I came here, but — nothing as wonderful as this."

"*Hai*, it's the same with me. I don't say that as part of my routine," he added, humor and embarrassment blending in his voice.

"I suppose I should ask now about seeing you again?" she said. She was startled by her own boldness.

"Um, I'm here almost every fourth day. You wouldn't have to pay either, except...management insists."

Angelica fell silent, thinking about the future. It would be even better next time, since she wouldn't be so scared. Already an impulse to caress him danced through her hands. Damik was an incomparable lover; she wanted to do it again with him....

On the other hand, there were all those other intriguing men out there whom she could try....

Luckily, her research was going to require staying on this planet for many, many months.

Big Ed

Isadora Alman

I had a new man in my life. Ed was a huge and hairy Mountain Man, a drawler and a brawler from Chickamauga, Tennessee. We were still somewhat new to each other, but we seemed to be going by the book. First the history: home town, education, work, interests, and now we were getting down to the cast of characters in the novels of our lives. I was telling him about my friendship/love affair with Dick, and was getting to a good part, the exciting three-way with Erik at the Russian River a year ago. He took the genuine corncob pipe on which he was chewing out of his mouth and said, "You mean the two fellers got it on too?"

"Well, each of us did with each of us eventually. That's one of the things that was so wonderful," I tried to explain.

"Sugar, you and that crowd of yours, you've been hanging around with too many fairy boys," he said, putting aside his pipe and pulling me against him. I sighed. What an expression! But what could you expect from a Good Old Southern Boy (I have prejudices of my own)?

I began, I thought gently, to broaden his world view. "Ed, if

40

a man appreciates the body of another man...." He toppled me onto my back and lifted my legs over his mammoth shoulders, lowering his head, something I guarantee will interrupt the most impassioned of monologues.

"C'mere, sugar, and let me appreciate your body." His voice was...shall we say, muffled, and I was glad that some of the other California practices were not unknown in the back woods of Tennessee.

Later, when I was cuddled against his matted chest I tried again. "You know, Ed, bisexual sensibilities don't make one less of a man or less of a woman. I rather think they make one more of what one is. Do you find me womanly?"

One of his huge hands was fondling my breast, hefting the weight of it in his palm. "Oh, sugar, how can you ask that?"

"Would you think me less so if I told you that when we're joined together I sometimes fantasize that I'm the one with the penis, that I'm fucking you, taking you with all the strength and sureness that is traditionally male?" As I talked, his left hand moved along my body, found another place it liked, and lingered. With his right hand he began stroking himself.

I became aware of a soft deep rumble of words, so I stopped talking to listen. "What a big cock, what a good strong cock," he was whispering. I closed my eyes and felt his fingers more intensely as they rubbed me to hardness, and realized that his soft words were underscoring the fantasy that I had been weaving — that big hand moving up and down, the heat and intensity gathering in my groin as the words of praise filled my head. "What a big hard cock you have," he was telling me. "I love feeling your cock grow hard."

We climaxed at the same time and it was better than Fourth of July fireworks. "Oh, Ed," I gasped. "I never...I...that was so...."

"Hush, sugar, I know. I know about the man and the woman in all of us. I truly do. Rest now. I've got some thinkin' to do."

I lay quietly beside him enjoying the calm, the huge hairy maleness of his bulk, the smell of his man's sweat and juices that filled the bed. "I'm goin' to take a shower, Jane," he said shortly.

"Can't I join you?"

"No. You go on into the other room. I'll join you in a while."

Well, some people are funny after sex. They feel sad or need to commune with higher powers or something. Maybe I touched some secret chord with our talk or our play, and he needed time to absorb it. I sat on the back porch, listening to some funky blues on the radio, and thought my own thoughts. Time passed, what seemed like a lot of time. I hadn't heard the sound of running water in a while.

"Ed?" I called.

"In a minute, Jane." And then in a few more minutes, "Jane?"

"I'm on the porch."

"Close your eyes!" His voice, usually so deep and rumbly, sounded different somehow, like sexy whispers in bed, softer and more Southern. "I want you to meet Edna."

I opened my mouth to ask questions — where? who?, or to be sociable if I had to, even though I was in my bathrobe. Then, as I opened my eyes, my mouth fell wide open too. I wasn't the only one wearing one of my bathrobes. Actually, Ed had on one of my hostess gowns — a long flowing pink silk affair that tied on one shoulder and was split along the opposite side to reveal the leg. The leg it revealed, I was relieved to see, remained un-shaven. So was his chest, and the thick beard I admired was still in place. (My shower drain would have been in big trouble if it were otherwise.) Such an extremely hairy man, and so much of him.

His longish hair was swept to the side and held with a bar-rette. His blue eyes were made bluer by the same shade of eye shadow and lash darkener. What there was to be seen of his cheeks above his beard glowed with a high pink blush. His mouth was lipsticked. A long strand of my pearls encircled his thick neck tightly like a choker. The nails on his hands were bright red, and from the way that he held them away from his body, apparently still wet with polish. The pantyhose in my dresser, purchased to fit me, a much shorter person, did not reach to his waist. This was revealed by the line low down on his groin which showed through the straining seams of the pink silk.

"Edna?" I understood, of course, that Edna was a part of Ed, like a spiritual twin sister sharing his body. I thought, too, of the part in the movie *Cabaret* where Joel Grey sings a love song to a gorilla dressed in a net tutu. It was a funny scene, immensely touching. I still hadn't said a word and realized that it was up to me to do so.

"Edna?" A nod of response. "Come and let me look at you!"

The huge stockinged feet padded out onto the porch. Well, what were a few splinters on such a momentous occasion. But the height difference. How could I deal with a Romeo and Juliet balcony scene? I took the hand held daintily away from the body and, mindful of the possibly wet polish, gently led the way back into the house and onto the couch. With Edna seated and me standing, the scene would play more appropriately. I poured some wine into a glass and held it out. We both sipped in silence. The glasses were then set aside. I leaned down and placed a gentle kiss on the wet and sweetly sticky lips. My hand rested on the exposed shoulder momentarily and then caressed its way beneath the folds of the pink silk bodice. I took a deep breath and my voice came out in a husky whisper. "What lovely smooth breasts you have, how soft and silky and firm."

The response was a satisfied sigh, "Ah, yes, sugar."

Shades of Grey

Jennifer Pruden

She is sitting on the steps of my apartment building when I get home from work. She cradles her black helmet between thighs clad in black wool. One broad yellow band in an otherwise black shirt clings to her breasts. The biking gloves I bought for her rest inside the helmet. Her blonde hair is pulled back in two barrettes from her wide cheekbones and brown eyes.

I shift the Filene's bag from one hand to the other in search of my house keys. I have three separate key rings: for work, for my car, for my apartment. At last I find them and insert the key into the lock, wriggling it as it makes uncertain progress. Sometimes it takes five minutes before I can get the door open. Today it is cooperative.

She stands waiting beside me, her helmet caught by its straps over her arm, her bicycle balanced beside her, waiting to be carried the three flights to my apartment. It is dry out today so there will be no mud streaks on the stairwell walls to be wiped down. She is breathing hard as I look at her, smiling, the point of my tongue just parting my lips.

I hold the door as she hoists the bike through and starts up the stairs. I watch her ass as she walks up the stairs, her cleats tapping. I watch the muscles move in the backs of her thighs, rippling black fabric.

"I brought you a present," I tell her back. She turns to look at me, smiles. I grin.

"Well," she says, "You're up to no good."

"Brat." I reach out, slip my hand between her thighs to caress her. "Is she hungry?"

"Mmm, you know she is...." She quickens her pace, then stands aside to let me unlock the door to my apartment. The door unlocks easily but I stand, waiting, with the key in the lock. I set the Filene's bag down and start to unbutton my blouse. She hisses at me until I pick up the bag and unlock the door.

"You have to have a bath first," I tell her.

"Oh, do I?" she answers.

"Yes!" I try to put a stern look on my face, but she leans over to kiss me. "That's enough of that right now," I say. She puts her bicycle in the hall and I take her helmet and gloves. I set them on the table by the door.

"Will I have the pleasure of your company in my bath?" she asks me.

"Not this time," I tell her. "Get yourself a towel."

I can hear her moving around in my bedroom as I go to draw her bath. I listen as she undresses. My breathing gets heavier as I imagine watching her. I love the curve where her thigh meets her belly, the shape of the muscle there, the softness of her inner elbow, the line of breast to armpit. I pour a packet of bath salts under the tap and watch the steam rise from the surface of the water, watch as the water is obliterated by a carpet of bubbles.

She tries not to make any noise as she walks into the bathroom, but the hairs on the back of my neck whisper of her movements.

I rise and turn to take the towel from her. I kiss her, her lips, her eyes, her neck. I take one earlobe into my mouth, then move to the other. "I'll be back shortly," I tell her. "Wait until I come back before getting into the bath." She rewraps herself in the towel.

I walk into my room. Her cycling clothes are neatly folded at the foot of my bed. The cedar of the chest lightly scents the air. I undress slowly, take my time hanging my clothes in the closet.

I pick up the few clothes that are lying around. I pull on my robe and belt it loosely.

She is leaning, wrapped in the towel, against the wall. "Okay, lady," I say. "Give me your towel." She unwraps herself. She takes her time. I hang the towel on the hook on the back of the door. "You can get in now," I tell her.

I take a washcloth from the closet and drape it over the edge of the tub, roll up the sleeves of my robe and dip the cloth in the water. I unwrap a new bar of soap and lather up the washcloth. I take one of her hands in mine and wash her arm. I soap her back. I wash her breasts, her thighs, her feet. I rinse her off leisurely. I wash her face for her. I rinse it off, and kiss the water from her eyelids. "Stand up," I tell her. I take the towel from the hook and begin to pat her dry.

"What is the surprise?" she asks me. "Was it in the bag you had?"

"Yes," I tell her. "Yes. Follow me." I bow and gesture toward the door.

"May I have the towel?" she asks. I have returned it to the hook.

"No. Just come with me."

"Any time," she whispers.

Smiling, I follow her into my room. The Filene's bag sits in the middle of my bed. She looks at me, then at the bag. She stands on the rug beside my bed. Her feet sink into the plush so I can see only the tops of them. I open the bag and reach in while I watch her. She looks at the bag, then at me. Our breasts rise and fall in unison.

I pull out four boxes and place them in a row on the bed. "I am going to open them for you," I tell her. I take the small flat box, and sit on the edge of the bed in front of her. I take the lid off and slowly unfold the layers of tissue. They rustle beneath my fingers. From this box I draw a pair of light grey stockings. They are silk, seamed. They wrap themselves around my fingers. She says nothing, just looks at them, at me.

"Give me your foot," I tell her. She places one foot in my out-stretched hand. I rest it on my knee as I roll up one stocking. I smooth it up her leg, adjusting the seam. I place her foot back on the floor, roll up the other stocking, and hold out my hand to receive warm, unclad skin. I bend down and brush her arch with my lips, breathing warmth against her skin. I lick and nibble at her arch until she leans over, places her hands on my shoulders, and moans. Only then do I slide the stocking over her foot, calf, knee, up her thigh. I place her foot back on the rug. She looks at me, eyes slightly glazed. I know that mine are the same.

I take the second box. My fingers search through tissue as I continue to watch her. I pull out a garter belt. It too is grey, but deep charcoal, almost black. I hold it out. No words are needed. She steps into it and I pull it up to her waist, fasten the stockings and trace the lines of the belt, the straps, with my fingers, then with my lips. I moan as her fingers travel my hairline, root through my hair, tangling, seeking. She begins to push me back on the bed but I stop her as I feel the corner of a box cut into my back, a reminder that I have not finished. I place my hand against her cheek, and she stands, swaying.

The third box contains a pair of shoes. They are soft suede, charcoal, high heeled. She gives me her foot. I place it in the shoe and set it down. She grasps my shoulder for balance as she picks up her other foot. The spike heels sink into the carpet.

She stands in front of me. She sways a little, trying to keep her balance. I run one finger around the top of her stocking, then up the inside of the thigh. I trace her lips with my finger. I slip it inside her, probing, then bring it to my lips to taste her sweetness. "One last box," I tell her as her body involuntarily follows my finger's retreat. "One. Last. Box." I can barely speak. Her nearness threatens to rob me of any thought that is not of her. I reach behind me. This is the largest box. I lift the lid and again unfold layers of paper, this time in haste. I hold up a robe for her. More grey silk. This time, an in-between shade. I stand and move behind her. I slip the robe up to her shoulders and leave it untied.

"Turn around," I tell her. I draw my breath in with a hiss, almost a gasp. "Go look in the mirror," I say, barely able to get the words out. "Do you like it?" She answers by coming to stand in front of me. Our bodies sway toward each other. She guides one of my hands between her legs. Her wetness is all the answer I need.

I remove the boxes from the bed, no longer concerned with neatness. Tissue hisses against itself as I sweep the boxes to the floor. I pull her on top of me as I lie back on the bed. Both our robes are open, breasts rub against breasts as we kiss. My hand creeps across her buttocks and down between her legs. She moans into my mouth as I enter her, first one finger, then a second and a third. Her thigh presses against my clitoris. She raises herself up, her knees at my waist, the garters straining as she moves across my belly. I reach up underneath her robe with my other hand to caress her nipples, rolling them between thumb and forefinger.

"May I go down on you?" I ask. I always ask her when we make love if I may eat her.

"Oh, please," she moans to me, already changing positions. My fingers do not lose their place within her. We are two fish sliding against each other in shallow water. I lean down between her legs to taste her, my fingers continuing their progress, making smooth sucking noises.

I love the taste of her. I rub my face against her lips as they open beneath me, blooming. I moan into her as her foot finds its way between my legs. I tighten my thighs around her ankle and my hips find the rhythm of hers. My arms slide under her legs to pull her against my mouth. I can no longer tell the difference between the noises we make: which are hers and which are mine?

Her clit moves beneath my tongue. As she begins to come, I follow. The surface of my skin has expanded and each touch of silk, of skin, of suede, sends me further out until I am too far to call back. We finish with a passion that will leave bruises.

I crawl up her body to lie on top of her. We kiss, and she licks herself from my face. We kiss again and I bury my face in her shoulder. We float off into sated sleep with small noises of contentment.

Later we wake briefly. She places the shoes on the floor, and we crawl beneath the blankets, skin warming skin. We curl around each other, two small animals curved body to body, breast to back. We sleep again.

Work and Play in the New Age

Marcy Sheiner

A few years ago, I was working for New Age Enterprises, a company that operated a mail order catalog of consumer goods for the "hip" generation — everything from camping gear to vitamins. The whole idea had been conceived and executed by one Jason Banks, a guy who had dropped out in the late '60s but had returned to the corporate world with all his business sense intact. I was Jason's secretary, or, to put it more accurately, his office wife.

Jason fascinated me from the start. Despite his soft, gentle manner, he exuded authority and, without much effort, got people to do what he wanted. For instance, although the pay scale at New Age was scandalously low, Jason managed to inspire his staff to put in incredibly long hours through a combination of wit, charm, and sophisticated double talk. Because he himself was such a workaholic, Jason's employees felt guilty if they didn't work more than eight hours a day.

No one was ever paid for overtime, but no one seemed to

mind; the highlight of the week came, in fact, when Jason would put down his pen late at night, lean back in his chair, and begin speaking in his soft, melodious voice. Slowly the workers, most of whom were bright, attractive women, would stop whatever they were doing and gather around Jason's chair. The subject could be almost anything, from the operation of the company to the results of the latest local election; it didn't matter what Jason spoke about, he commanded instant attention.

Although I spent my first few months on the job trying to observe all this with objectivity, I was not immune to Jason's charms. He wasn't exactly good-looking, but his sea-green eyes held my attention. His lean, hard, and energetic body rarely suggested sexual overtures; rather, it seemed that the manner in which Jason assumed control was what excited women most.

As the months progressed, I became less and less analytical about Jason, and more and more responsive to his needs. I would find myself anticipating his wishes: pulling a file before he asked for it, ordering his lunch without his suggesting it, bringing him little gifts of fruit and home-baked cookies. He was always extremely appreciative, and he constantly praised my work, which spurred me on to do more for him. I would happily work until after midnight, even if it meant cancelling a date. I learned to adjust my schedule to adapt to Jason's. I wanted only to give to this man who worked so hard and for whom I had so much respect.

Gradually my sexual desires entered the picture. Jason would be dictating a letter, and I'd lose a whole sentence, imagining his hands on my breasts. Or he'd sit next to me to show me something, and the hair on my arms would become electrified by his nearness. Or we'd be walking down the hall, Jason hurrying along as always, me running after him, and I'd suddenly be seized with the urge to run my hands along his hips, an urge so powerful I thought I'd faint with the effort to restrain myself.

When I wasn't working for Jason I was dreaming of him, sweet warm dreams in which we slept naked beside each other. Or I was masturbating, fantasizing about him fucking me on the office couch, my desk, standing behind a closed door. I knew it could be a total disaster to fuck the boss. I weighed the arguments pro and con day and night. I stopped seeing other men, girlfriends, my family. I never went anywhere except to work. I no longer had any other interests in life: Jason Banks had become my obsession.

One night he and I were working late. Everyone else had miraculously gone home.

"Let me see the layout of page twelve," Jason ordered from across the room.

I fetched the copy and brought it to him, noticing that his shoulders were hunched with tension. Without thinking about it, I followed my instinct and began massaging his neck and shoulders. He moaned softly as I rubbed and kneaded his stiff muscles. After a few minutes I realized that I was touching Jason in more than a friendly manner. I knew that I should stop, but I couldn't. I loved him, and felt so devoted to him, that I wanted nothing more in all the world than to serve him, to ease all his troubles and pain.

I let my hands move down along his arms, sighing as I ran them over his biceps, then rubbed my fingers along his spine, massaging each vertebra. Love poured through my body and flowed out through my hands. I could have massaged Jason all night without ever tiring. He turned and put his arms around me. My breasts were level with his mouth, and he unhesitatingly opened my blouse to suck on them.

He led me to the couch across the room, lay me down and undressed me. I spread my legs and plunged my fingers into my steaming cunt, watching Jason's response. He unzipped his pants and pulled them off. I'd often wondered what Jason would look like naked. Because he was skinny, I'd feared he'd have a small prick. I needn't have worried. Jason's cock was big and hard, and now it throbbed and pulsated inches from my face. He remained standing, holding his penis with one hand while I lapped at it like a hungry little puppy. But I could see how hard it was for Jason to relax, so I sat up and pushed him gently onto the couch, forcing him to lie back while I attended to him.

A workaholic to the end, Jason couldn't just lie back and allow himself to be pleasured. He kept touching my clit, my tits, almost as if he felt an obligation to do so.

"Jason," I said, jumping up. "Stay right here. Don't move. I'll be back in a minute." I dashed down the hall to the supply closet, found a long piece of rope and ran back to him.

"What are you doing?" he asked, only half protesting, as I began tying his hands together.

"I'm going to force you to allow me to give you pleasure. Without your lifting so much as a finger."

His lips crinkled at the corners in a half-smile. I finished tying his hands, then bound his ankles together. Finally, I picked up my silk scarf and rammed it into his astonished mouth. I stood back for a moment to survey my handiwork: there on the couch lay my boss, completely helpless, completely at my mercy. For once, Jason Banks was powerless.

I resumed my ministrations to his cock, which had grown at least an inch as a result of his captivity. I luxuriated in the opportunity to take my time, and licked his prick over and over from shaft to head before actually taking it into my mouth and sucking. When I finally did, I pushed it as far down my throat as it would go. As I sucked, I ground my hips and clit against Jason's leg, getting hotter and wetter until, as I sensed he was about to spill his hot cum into my mouth, I came. I needed to have him inside my cunt, and hurriedly sat on top of him, shoving his cock in to the hilt. He groaned, a low throaty animal sound muffled by the scarf. His eyes, the only outlet for his feelings, bulged, as his cock shot load after load of cum, bathing my cunt with its thick sweet juices.

I moaned as a second orgasm overtook me. My tits ached to be squeezed; since Jason's hands were tied, I had to do it myself. The sight of me coming, squeezing my own stiff nipples, must have driven him wild, because he immediately became erect again and, struggling within the confines of his bindings, thrust his pelvis vigorously up and down until he came once more, shooting into my welcoming belly. Finally I collapsed on top of him and, raining tender kisses upon his face, removed the scarf from his mouth. He used his new freedom to kiss me in appreciation and whispered, "Next time I'll tie you up."

I didn't care who tied up whom, just that there be a next time. And so there was. The next morning, Jason circulated a memo saying that since the company couldn't afford to pay overtime, he was instituting a policy that everyone leave at five sharp. Thereafter we fucked every night, in every possible location: on the desk, in the swivel chairs, on the floor, standing up in his closet, or behind the toilet stall. He tied me to the chair; I chained him to the desk.

Meanwhile, the staff, losing interest in the company without Jason's midnight talks, began to find better-paying jobs elsewhere. To cut costs, Jason and I moved in together and began running the business from home. Eventually we expanded our catalog to include a full line of sexual toys, every one of which is personally pretested by the President and Vice-President of New Age Enterprises.

Love Object

A. Gayle Birk

I have been told about and read about the one I must find and make mine. She has been described as electrifying, pulsating, and totally undemanding. I continued trying to convince myself that to be with her would fill the empty spaces in my life. To be touched by one such as her could mean an end to lonely, endless weekends without touch or conversation. I should find someone to bring me into life as I imagined I wanted to be, to turn to, to give to, take from, and be accepted by for myself. Long ago I resigned from the world. I simply could not relate to those who made demands.

My fantasy sustains me. The thought of meeting the one so deliciously described to me, one I am assured will come to me if I just make it happen, is almost more than I can stand. My vagina becomes wet and warm, my skin feels soft, touchable, and my eyes look brighter as I smile at my mirror reflection. Looking at my body is not an overwhelming event, but I explore it sometimes and even let go enough to stroke my breasts, my pubic hair, my buttocks. The sensation pleases me, but I never thought I could give myself pleasure; there has to be another, perhaps the one described to me by my two friends — my only friends.

When they first told me about this beauty I blushed. They laughed. They said to be touched by one so giving could at first be an embarrassment, but that would be short-lived when it became apparent that my passion would not possess me, and would not have to be called upon unless I so desired it. This lovely, my friends assured me, was the kind that we falsely convince ourselves could never make us happy. One who gives only when asked, who makes no demands and who brings ecstasy and delight as you rise to the height of tidal-wave orgasm.

"God," I thought, "I must experience this." But first I had to put aside my guilt for dreaming of fulfillment. My mother told me that sexual desires were sinful, that women were created to please men and would probably never be pleased themselves. I believed her for a long time.

In my quest to get a better education than my forebears, I realized I had lost my desire to communicate. I was tired. I could not cope with demands, so turned off my valves — sexual and social — to work, to study, to be alone and fashion my future. At twenty-six, I am loved by no one, really, except my lonely mother and my two friends who jarred the cogs of my mind regarding the delights of loving without commitment.

My two friends are lesbians, as I believe myself to be. My lifestyle chose me because I knew as it was, my life was a lie. For a long time I have had deep feelings for women, but have never been gently touched. I am afraid and my friends continue to help me find myself. I experience moments of desiring sexual encounters, and those moments are usually in a half-awake, half-asleep state when I realize I am touching myself, caressing myself. The thought of having another's hands on me makes me cringe. Hands want something and I have convinced myself I don't have what might make them happy.

When I shared my feelings with my two friends, they assured me that one day I must meet the one who could help alter such feelings. They told me where to find such a lovely. They assured me that I will be in control — like flicking a switch. I can have her or not have her at my will and she will give to me until I am done. These thoughts have swirled around in my head for many weeks. I finally told them I would seriously consider their suggestion.

I did. I went out just last evening to the place where they said I would find her. And, God, they spoke the truth. She was just a few feet away. I worked myself toward her hoping no one noticed the effect she was having on me. Wouldn't my friends be pleased. Then I was standing so close to her, I could touch her if I chose. But I tried to appear impervious as I stole glances when I knew no one was looking. The place was about to close so few people remained. Boldly I reached out and touched her. Did she smile?

When I walked out of the store she was with me. I had done it! I had asserted myself for something I was convinced would make me happy. I have what I deserve — Vi my new lover; Vi my vibrator.

I snuggled her against my side, my firm grip assuring her safety. As I drove home anxiety replaced my excitement. Could I do what I had in mind to do? Could I risk vulnerability? I reasoned that Vi would not be capable of capturing me; I would control her just as my friends had promised. How could an inanimate object become the aggressor? No way, I assured myself. Nothing and no one could ever do that to me. I was strong. I had practiced being strong so no one, no thing, nothing, could turn me into a puppet.

When I arrived home, I grasped the package lying beside me and pressed it against my breast. My palms grew moist. Why was I so nervous, so frightened? She couldn't talk, she couldn't implore that I give her something I did not have to give.

I tightened my grip even more as I slid the key into the door lock. Still holding Vi, I latched and locked the door and went into my bedroom. I laid her on my bed and slowly and carefully removed her from the box. She had attachments. One for scalp, one for muscles, and one concave rubber attachment for fleshy parts of one's body. That was the one I wanted, I thought. Jesus, was it? My friends forgot that part of their seductive description of Vi. I knew who was who in American history and English literature, but when it came to my own body, I knew little more than location and functions of its parts.

Vi had two speeds. I would start with the low one. One must crawl before one walks. I screwed in the attachment I had assigned as the correct one, then carefully lay Vi on the bed and plugged in her cord. I stared at her as I unzipped my jeans and let them fall around my ankles. I stopped. Did I want to do this?

Again, moisture covered my palms. I must. I stepped out of my jeans and kicked them aside. I moved Vi over and lay beside her. I took her in my right hand, flicked her switch to low and gently placed her against my abdomen. Then millimeter by millimeter, I moved her toward the place I feared would expose vulnerability.

When the rubber concavity touched my clitoris, I gasped and drew her away from me. Then, gently I replaced her, applying no pressure for a few seconds to allow the vibration to play around and occasionally touch my swelling clitoris. My toes flexed, my legs jerked involuntarily. Vi was teasing me. Damn it, she was calling the shots!

No way. I controlled me, my feelings, my responses. I pressed the concavity onto my clitoris. My legs became rigid, my throat constricted. My intellect told me to stop, my human needs ignored the pleas.

My entire body went into a rigor. I relaxed. I dropped Vi. She hummed beside me. I rolled over on my back. Muscles relaxed, I felt a smile form on my lips. Oh, lord. Relaxed. No one talking, not even me. Minutes or perhaps hours passed. I grasped Vi and again she gave me pleasure. Again. Again.

When I glanced at the clock just before falling asleep I noted the time. Midnight. Machine again had won over "man" — woman. Maybe someday a real woman instead of Vi, a real woman instead of my fantasy lover.

Read Me A Story

Kathy Dobbs

Over and over, my concentration wandered from my lover's lips as the noise outside continued. Damn those kids, I thought, as my tongue instinctively answered Sheila's warm mouth. At the same time she was getting heated up, I was getting close to the end of my rope.

"Could we put some music on?" I asked quietly, trying not to break the mood she was swimming in. It took a second for the words to register; it wasn't always easy to jump from sex mode to reality on such short notice. Suddenly she nodded, and got up off the bed. I took the opportunity to use the bathroom and get a drink of water. For some reason, I just couldn't let myself go tonight. I needed, and indeed wanted, to immerse myself in the mood, the sensuality she and I had together, but I was having trouble even getting my feet wet. Sheila noticed my distraction when I came back into the room.

"Is something wrong?" I was almost afraid to say anything, not wanting to disappoint her. Lovemaking was always beautiful between us. But I knew I couldn't escape her inquisitive eyes.

"Well, I just can't...those damn kids out there...I don't

know...." I stumbled over myself, sitting down next to her beautiful outstretched body. I idly laid my hand on her breast, liking the way the soft flesh felt under my palm.

"Why don't we have a drink?" she suggested.

A few moments later we were naked on the couch, wine glasses in hand. The cool pink liquid warmed my throat. I liked this room of our apartment best. Done in deep blues and browns, it was always the darkest room in the house. Now it was lit with candles and soft-light lamps; the smell of burning jasmine incense was pleasant but not overwhelming. I allowed myself to relax, trying to forget all the things running through my head — what we needed to pick up at the store, bills we needed to mail, things left unfinished. My mind was on the verge of blankness when I spotted the book on the coffee table.

As a couple, Sheila and I were perfectly matched — we both had a passion for the new and exciting, and erotica was no exception. We indulged in new toys, vibrators, creams, even racy comic books. Now I picked up the small freebie paperback that had come with the last shipment from our favorite mail-order sex catalogue. I hadn't even bothered to look at this one, having been sorely disappointed with the last book, which had an equally corny title. These books were written by men, whose views of sex, and of women's sexuality in particular, never ceased to amaze me. My opinion of their ideas might have been biased because I am a lesbian; but I had slept with men, and had found it ridiculous how many of the important details of lovemaking these writers left out.

My lover was at the other end of the couch, reading some magazine. I opened the book. She glanced over at me and smiled. The book's title was *Stud On The Loose,* and the front cover showed a young girl with everything spilling out of her T-shirt. As I began to read, I found that the main character didn't waste any time getting laid.

So, do you want to get fucked? asked Mr. Stud of one of his many lovers. I thought it rather silly of him to ask, seeing that he had her tied spread-eagled on the bed with a gag in her mouth. He didn't wait for an answer as he took his place and plunged into her. Though it was difficult to be sure of her opinion, he obviously thought she was enjoying herself, and continued to thrust into her.

Yes...yes don't stop. Oh, he feels so good inside me. I can feel his cock head against my tight muscles as he pulls himself all the way out then plunges in again...ummmm. Deeper, yes, deeper. Hard, hard, pump me pump me pump that hard cock of yours into my pussy, baby....

He stopped. With his cock still buried deep inside her, he stopped. Reaching over, he untied her legs one at a time. He gave her a quick slap on the thigh and turned her over, her ass in the air, on her knees.

Something inside me stirred, deep. I felt the girl's anticipation deep inside my own body. I knew what he would do, and I knew how it would feel, and I wanted it.

He reached around to her breasts, taking them in his hands, his stiff penis pushing against her ass cheeks. His fingers took hold of her nipples, rubbing and squeezing, and she moaned deeply.

I could feel it. I could feel the stabs of pleasure running through her body, exploding in her clit. Waves of sweet honey ran through her, through me. It wasn't until my free hand brushed against the book that I noticed it was my own fingers rubbing my nipples, sending warm stirrings to my own womanhood. I continued reading, and rubbing....

Yes, you like that, don't you? I bet your pussy is so hot for my prick. Can you feel it? Can you feel my cock against you? Oh, but you want it inside you, don't ya, baby. You on your knees with your cute ass up in the air, your pussy just dripping wet and wanting it. Yes, yes...

Yes, yes please...his hands on my ass, kneading my cheeks with his strong hands...something warm and wet on my ass, licking, yes his tongue...oh, ooh.

He licked her ass, paying special attention to the tight flesh of her asshole, feeling her tense up as he plunged the tip of his tongue into her, then loosen. She moaned as he worked it in circles, in and out. He knew how wet her pussy would be once he entered her. And when his cock wouldn't let him hold off any longer, he plunged.... You like it slow? So you can feel all nine inches of me enter you? Or fast? Fast and deep...oh, listen to her moan....

He put his hands on her waist and pulled her back onto his hard cock again and again, fast...then slow, letting her juices overflow onto his pubic hair as he was deep inside her. And he kept on pumping....

No, don't stop...each thrust sweeter and sweeter...getting stronger...it's getting so close...I'm going to come with him fucking me like this, so hard and so fast....

And they came. In one big flourish, that climactic moment when the blood pounds in your ears and your body starts to tingle. It starts at your toes, and climbs, and explodes through you. Wave after wave of delight, your body tensing and relaxing, rising and falling. That point beyond reality, beyond consciousness, when the world disappears and all that matters is the supreme intensity of the orgasm overtaking your body, your mind....

I wanted to feel those waves. I wanted to crash against the shore of an orgasm and let it take me.

As the plot of the book simmered down, and Mr. Stud was on his way to finding another girl to lay, I realized I had been nearly holding my breath during their lovemaking, and I let out a sigh. Sheila looked over at me, smiled, then noticed my hand still on my breast, gently massaging it.

"Was it good?" she asked quietly, nearly whispering. Her smile told me of her amusement, but her eyes registered passion. I felt slightly foolish, and blushed. Her eyes were growing intense. I smiled quickly and went back to my book. There were times, such as this, when the intensity of her stare was too much even for me.

So once again I joined Mr. Stud on his hunt. But he barely had his new conquest undressed when I felt Sheila's hand on my leg. Every one of her five fingers sent its own message to my body. Each place her hand touched tingled. I was amazed and excited, and I looked up at her. She was still reading her magazine, a mood of nonchalance about her. It seemed she had no idea what her touch was doing to me. Yet she felt my eyes on her, and smiled.

"Go on, keep reading." She said it quietly, sweetly, but with an edge of control. It was an order, and I turned my eyes back to the page in front of me.

As Mr. Stud buried his face between his new girl's legs, she moaned for him to lick her sweet, swollen clit. Her breathing quickly turned to panting, her moans grew more insistent. I was beginning to pant a little myself as the action continued, for behind the black and white of the page were my lover's fingers, edging up my legs, closer and closer to that ache between them. My fingers moved from one nipple to the other, painting circles on my erect points with my fingertips. The sensations became overwhelming, and I closed my eyes, letting out a soft moan to show my pleasure. Sheila's voice startled me.

"Keep reading. Out loud." I opened my eyes in surprise. Surely she was joking. But her face showed no amusement. There was not even the hint of a smile on her lips, and her eyes were demanding. I realized that she was serious.

"I can't...I mean, you're not really..." I stopped in mid-sentence, my mouth hanging open. As stupid as I must've looked, she didn't smile. Her eyes grew even colder, and her hand on my inner thigh began to tighten.

"Do it," she replied quietly, adding a quick pinch to her grip. I wasted no time in beginning my recitation. I knew from experience that she wouldn't hesitate to spank me, bringing her hand down hard on my exposed ass. So I read....

His tongue flicked over her clit, back and forth. He could taste her juices, sweet and warm, and worked his tongue in and out of her entrance. She moaned, squirming on the couch. Suddenly he put his hands underneath her thighs and lifted her up so that his tongue was now in her ass. She cried out, but as his tongue continued to push into her, her cries became moans of pleasure. Her fingertips brushed her clit, and she began stroking her aching need....

I had to stop, if for nothing else but to catch my breath. As I read, Sheila had spread my legs wide, and now her fingers were inside my wetness, rubbing circles on my own hard clitoris. The sensations were so strong I had to close my eyes and give in to them. But when she noticed the interruption she stopped her movement. I looked up into her angry eyes. One again I turned to the page.

He reached down and began unzipping his jeans, releasing his huge, stiff cock. Watching her get herself off had made him as horny as ever, and he could barely wait to put his dick inside her. She looked startled as she caught the first glance of his organ. He was proud of his nine inches, and the way he knew how to use them.

He positioned himself between her legs, taking his cock in his hand and moving it along her wet slit, rubbing her clit with the purple swollen head. She was moaning for him to enter her, and he suddenly obliged, thrusting his full length into her with one quick motion. She very nearly screamed....

I could no longer go on; for as Mr. Stud entered his teenage prey, my lover had plunged three fingers into my very wet and aching pussy. She pumped in and out hard, deep, and I dropped the book onto the floor. This time she didn't make me continue. She knew I was too far gone with her fucking me. My hips began rising in rhythm with her thrusts, pushing her even deeper.

"You want more, don't ya, babe?" she asked between my cries.

"Y-yes, pl-please...." I stuttered, not really wanting her to stop, but knowing that what she had in mind would be even better. She took my hand and laid it between my legs, urging me to rub my clit as she slipped into the bedroom. When she returned, I opened my eyes to see her holding one of our dildos, a nice eight inches glistening with lubricant. I sighed in anticipation, and she sat down between my legs and began rubbing the head along my lips.

She very slowly entered me, letting me feel all eight inches, until she reached my cervix. I had temporarily stopped playing with myself to enjoy the intense sensations as she again, very slowly, pulled it out. Her beat got faster, and my fingers helped build me to a frenzy. I could feel the waves of pleasure getting stronger and stronger.

Just as I felt right on the edge of my orgasm, she stopped. "I know you want it, baby. Turn over," she commanded softly. I obeyed, moving to my knees. The scene from the book flashed in my mind — the girl getting fucked doggy-style by Mr. Stud. The pictures in my head turned me on even more, as I anticipated the dildo entering me from behind.

I didn't have long to wait as Sheila got into position and thrust inside me. Her free fingers reached around to rub my clitoris, and I thought I would faint.

"Yes, baby, that's it. I want you to come for me. I want you to let it take you, sweetie," she said as she pumped faster. "Doesn't this nice hard cock feel good inside you? Yes, you like to get fucked from behind, don't you? Feels so good, so strong...."

It was coming closer. I could feel it. To me, it was like nearing the edge of a cliff, step by sweet step, until finally you reach it...and fall. I was falling. My body was shaking. There was always that moment of fear, the fear of forever falling, and she was always there to catch me. To hold me tight until the spasms stopped shaking me, to tell me she loved me and soothe my refreshed, dream-dazed body.

Wet Silk

Edna MacBrayne

The bronze doorbell was cast in the shape of a human breast. That small touch of wit calmed some of my apprehension, but to tell the truth, I was pretty much of a corporate-urban wreck. My colleagues saw my malaise long before I did, and must have dropped a hint or two close to the seat of power. The arrangements to bring me here were made quickly and with discretion. I was given no choice. "Just go," they said, "and you'll come back a new person."

The front door was open, letting in a warm breeze. I walked into the entry hall, and though not surprised at the elegance, found it reassuring. A magnificent Lachaise nude dominated the hall. It was the one of a figure with her arm raised, beckoning. It looked as light as milkweed and as perfect as an egg.

I heard the click of heels on the stone floor and saw an attractive woman come toward me. "Good morning," she said. "We're so glad to have you here." Her manner was that of someone who thoroughly enjoys entertaining. She gestured for me to follow her through an atrium filled with flowering plants and a small fountain. After leading me through a series of pleasantly disorienting corridors, she opened a door and ushered me into a room. "This is where you can change and relax. You'll find robes in the closet and we'll bring you some refreshments." As she was going out the door, she added, "Take as much time as you want, and when you're ready, go outside and follow the path." Then she took my hand in hers, and said, with a smile that would melt rock, "I hope you enjoy your stay here," and left.

The room was comfortable, furnished with restraint and care as elsewhere in the building. But I was still feeling awkward and nervous. It seemed a bit foolish to be all alone in the midst of this luxury. I was looking out through the wall of sliding glass when a nice looking fellow came into the room with a tray. "If you want anything more, please ring," he said, pointing to a bell, then disappeared before I could thank him.

Getting out of my clothes improved my attitude. I reached into the closet and pulled out a finely batiked kimono. It was as light as a breath. When I put it on it felt like nothing, except that the soothing silk against my skin made me shiver.

I sat down at the table and looked at the tray of food the young man had left me. A soft cheese oozed from its rind. There was paté, crusty bread, and a dish of black olives, as well as a small crystal vase holding pink anthuriums. I poured myself some champagne and felt myself beginning to lounge instead of sit. A grin formed in my toes and wiggled its way up to my face. I cut a chunk of the butter-smooth paté, spread it on some of the bread and bit into it.

With the glass of wine in hand, I walked over to the window to take a look outside. It was impossible to see the extent of the grounds, because of the profuse plantings of shrubs and flowers; however, I could make out two figures, one resting on the grass and the other diving into a natural pool. The scene was idyllic — and a little unnerving. I wondered if I would be able to trust them. I gulped some more wine and realized I was back to my old habits, so I sat down at the table again and nibbled a bit of cheese. I was careful to sip the champagne.

Life was better already. I was much more relaxed, but still the idea of taking a casual stroll outside wearing nothing but a thin robe, and then getting closely involved with two people I'd never met — well, that seemed more than a little alien to me. On the other hand, maybe it was time for me to loosen up, to let my life just happen. Besides, I was curious — and it had been paid for in advance.

This train of thought got me outside the glass doors and into the garden. It smelled wonderful. With only the silk brushing my skin, I was weightless and smooth as I walked to the garden pool.

The two of them were still as I had seen them from the window; one lounging on the grass and the other in the water. Neither wore any clothes.

"Come in for a swim," they invited me.

"How warm is it?" I asked, dreading the thought of cold water.

"It's perfect. If you don't believe it, test it with your toe."

I stuck my foot in. It was perfect. I let the kimono slide to the ground and waded in, surprised to find a sandy bottom. "Is it always this warm?" I asked, surrendering my body to the buoyancy.

"Winter and summer. It's fed by thermal jets. Like it?"

"It's heaven."

The one on the grass let out a sigh. "It's better than heaven because there's no harp music, but I'm confronted by the terrible decision of whether to stay here and roast or immerse myself in the cooling waters. Life is a burden."

"Why don't you be sociable? We have a guest," said the one in the water.

With that, the third body splashed into the pool. It wasn't a large pool. I expected there would be some tentative physical contact, but the light touches I felt were obviously inadvertent. I was pleased by this. It gave all three of us a chance for verbal play and a way to get to know each other. I was beginning to trust them already.

I felt my shoulders loosen and my foot spring with delight as it passed over one of the jets feeding water from the bottom. My progressive relaxation must have been obvious, because my playmates suggested that they give me a massage. That sounded inviting, so we got out of the pool, dried off, and then they led me to a padded ledge built out from the hillside. I hopped on and lay down on my stomach with the sun warming my back. I felt a trickle of liquid down my spine.

"We're using pure mineral oil for a very good reason. You'll find out later."

They rubbed oil into my skin from neck to feet and then began to search for knots of tension. It was a strange sensation. One of them started with my hands and the other with my feet; their intention being, I suppose, to meet somewhere in the middle. As they rubbed and kneaded I felt like a poorly mixed batch of bread dough, full of lumps. "Am I a basket case?" I mumbled.

"Your body is about as relaxed as a steel girder, but let's not talk now. We'll fix it."

They were gentle, but as they got rid of one group of lumps they'd go deeper and find more clusters of tight knots to annihilate with their persevering fingers. I lost track of time. I no longer felt like a giant loaf of bread. Now I was a dipper full of hot fudge sauce being poured on warm cake. I couldn't see what they were doing, but I could feel them moving around me, sometimes accidentally brushing my body with a forearm as they changed positions. There was an occasional swirl of hair against my skin and their touch became lighter, less probing.

Nothing mattered. I was boneless, weightless, and completely under their power.

Their shift in emphasis did not disturb me in the slightest as their playful hands explored my body. They pulled on my fingers and toes to test for any residual tension, and when they found none they began to tease me with their fingers. These were not caresses. There was still strength behind their touch, but the signal was not therapeutic anymore. One rubbed my shoulders while the other rubbed my calves. They acquainted me with bunches of nerve endings I never knew existed in my elbows and knees. Their touch was as delicate as a bubble. Mentally, I purred. I felt the onset of desire.

Thumbs glided down either side of my spine and went back up again. The palms of soft hands stroked the insides of my thighs, never going up as far as I hoped they would, but traveling all the way to my heels and toying with my ankles.

It went on forever. Time was lost, and space became small pockets of my flesh that kept melting.

When they resorted to using only their fingertips, I was fully aroused. I wanted them to climb all over me and cover my body with theirs. I needed their lips and tongues on me in a silky ooze of oil and saliva. My hand reached out to beg them for more, but in an unbroken, lingering stroke four hands coursed down my body. One of them said, "That's enough for now. We want you to join us in a light meal."

A soft moan escaped me. The last thing in the world I wanted was a light meal. I was in the mood for a royal feast of arms and legs and hips. I wanted tongues and lips and fingers, not cheese and crackers. The second one patted me on the rear end and said, "Come on. It'll be more fun than you think. Besides, we're thirsty."

I could hardly argue with that, so I pulled myself up and followed them to a linen tablecloth that had been spread on the grass. In the center of the cloth was a large lazy susan filled with bowls of food and bottles of drink. There were no plates, forks, spoons, or glasses.

"How are we supposed to eat?" I asked.

"Any way you like," they answered.

Each of them tipped bottles of mineral water into their mouths as I sank down on the tablecloth. I wanted to eat quickly and get back to where we had left off. Without much enthusiasm I picked up a spear of asparagus and chewed on it. Most of the food looked as though you would at least need a spoon to eat it.

"Here, try some chicken salad." A hand bearing what looked like a bunch of noodles appeared in front of my nose. "Open your mouth. You'll like it." I tilted my head back and tried to get most of it into my mouth. Inevitably, a few strands of noodles escaped and slithered down my chin. As I sucked them up I began to taste the wonderful combination of ginger, soy, garlic and bean thread. There were even a few morsels of chicken.

"It's delicious," I sputtered through a full mouth, "can I have a napkin?"

"There aren't any," came the reply.

Like a kid, I wiped my mouth and chin with the back of my hand and then rubbed it down my thigh. They both laughed and offered me some wine.

I was trying not to glug down the wine too rapidly when one of them said, "Hold out your hand." I did, and immediately found it garnished with a thick dollop of whipped cream. On top of that went a plump blackberry.

"Thank you," I said, and raised my arm to eat it off my hand. My palm had no sooner reached my mouth when I felt something touch my right nipple. It was a bit of mayonnaise. "Glue,"

I was informed. With this ingenious adhesive a small shrimp and a piece of parsley created a miniature still life on my chest. Still holding my handful of whipped cream, I heard one of them declare, "It's a genuine work of art."

"I agree," said the other one, "but it's asymmetrical. We should do the other side."

And so I was made symmetrical with additional mayonnaise, shrimp, and parsley. The designer said, "You know, that looks good enough to eat," and with lips and tongue, gobbled it off me.

"Aw, now you've ruined it," said the other one, plastering more glue on me and restoring the artful theft. Most of the shrimp was used up this way as I sat contentedly licking whipped cream off my hand while the two of them discussed the merits of my right and left nipples as flavoring agents for seafood or armatures for sculpture.

"The right one has a piquant taste and surprising firmness," proclaimed gourmand number one.

"The left one has a musky flavor and a superior spongy texture," argued art critic number two.

In an effort to settle the dispute they decided to test other areas of my body and requested that I lie down so they could continue their experiment. I was not opposed to this idea, so with a towel for my pillow, I spread myself full length on the tablecloth with another handful of cream and some fresh, ripe strawberries.

I was completely unaware that my body held the marvels now being discovered. My companions had begun to cooperate with each other by this time. They reminded me of shoppers comparing the quality of caviar or fine cheese.

"Have you tried stuffed mushrooms in crook of elbow?"

"No, I'm still testing meatballs in hollowed out shoulder." The mushroom one then sucked wine from my navel while the meatball aficionado spread pork in peanut sauce on my thigh. They took their time with every bite of food, prolonging the act of removing it from my skin with their lips and tongues.

"Now do you see why we insist on using mineral oil?"

"Whoever invented plates and cutlery was a cold, unfeeling wretch," commented the other.

I just lay there with a scrutable grin on my face, shuddering with pleasure as they did remarkable things to my knees with egg and olive salad. To be this passive while being amused and aroused all at the same time was something I never thought possible for myself. But here I was, a human platter watching two amiable and creative people nibble on me. I had a difficult time remaining still, especially when they began dessert.

Slowly they spooned the rest of the whipped cream onto the triangle between my legs. This they studded with fruit. They began to eat, delicately at first, making comments on the freshness of the fruit and the sweetness of the cream. It was all very correct. From the conversation, one almost would have thought we were at a formal dinner party.

Once the fruit was gone and there was nothing left but dripping cream rapidly losing its air content, they started to suck and slurp and use their fingers. I seemed to have hands and mouths all over me, charging my body with a special urgency. That fundamental rhythm, my heartbeat, grew stronger and quickened as if I were running. I clutched for a companion and one of them came to me in an embrace, kissing me with a passion that spoke of mutual arousal. We clung together and I squirmed with delight at feeling the completeness of a whole body next to me.

The fingers and tongues never stopped. They explored creases and crevices, hollows and bulges. They skittered across some areas and lingered, probing in others, inserting wands of pleasure unexpectedly. My body, the former serving platter, had been turned into a musical instrument being played by two accomplished artists.

I throbbed and tingled from the tender friction of their legs, fingers and lips. The groin of one pressed against mine with a solid beat. The tip of a tongue searched inside my nostril for a more sensitive membrane. Each of my hands held its fill of warm soft flesh that I ached to suck, but squeezed gently instead.

We had adopted a single rhythm, moving together. Our breath came faster as we ground our bodies furiously into each other's, rubbing, squeezing, licking, twisting this way and that to find the end solace for our need. Inhibitions abandoned and faces skewed in ecstasy, we pulsed our way past the plateau and rushed to leap into the liquid. Like three pieces of wet silk slithering together in a circle, we were one large organ bursting with a single melody. It roared through us, a cataclysm, about to drench us in release.

At last there was no holding back. We exploded into rich

spasms of flood-like orgasm, making us buck, tremble, and moan as the tension broke through our forms. We held on to the beauty we had created until we began to float, glide, and hover in a state of benign sanctity. Naked, simple, and free, we touched each other with reverence.

Our communion continued in quiet; our bodies now on the grass, dappled in shadows of leaves as the sun tracked its way across the sky. We curled into one another with small, reassuring pats, like children sleeping on the back porch in summer. None of us wanted to get up. The luxury of skin touching skin was still with us, not easily abandoned. With lazy pleading we finally persuaded the one closest to the beverages to reach for a bottle of water that we shared. Drinking necessitated sitting up and from there it was a quick step to dipping some towels into the pool so we could clean each other off. We agreed to a swim. While in the pool I realized that the day was far from over.

"What are we going to do after we get out of the pool?" I asked.

"Oh, we'll think of something," one replied knowingly.

"Yes," said the other, "but first we must have some tea."

The Sensuous Housewife

Bonnie Stonewall

I'm camping atop a cliff. The lawn chair I'm holding down with my butt is the only one around to remain upright during this latest weather tantrum folks here call the Santa Ana wind. Nature seems to go into a daily snit for a few hours in the afternoon. Perhaps in protest of humanity's crass disregard of the blessings of this earth, the Santa Ana sees to it that anything that isn't rooted to the ground is swept away into the abyss. The rugged beauty of this spot is, unfortunately, a last vestige of natural splendor in an area that has been raped by weekend "naturalists." Pavement, motorboat launches, and waterslides have managed to supplant deer trails, the lone canoe, and the thundering waterfall. The land is pockmarked with tents and RVs — the Los Angeles of public campgrounds. As I sit here alone in my summer vacation estrangement, I wonder what a sensualist is to do but retreat into fantasy?

It's become a silly game I play while my husband and children are off fishing or swimming or hiking — trying to decide which of the three T-shirts I've brought on this retreat will make me — a bisexual housewife and mother — most identifiable to the others at the campground. I hope they'll perceive me as I perceive them — the honeymoon couple, the pretty blonde in white shorts brushing her teeth at the water pump, the fiery brunette with the scarlet talons at the cash register in the convenience store, the two lady cops outside the police station. They're all hot for it! I know it, I know it! The wheel of fortune in my mind plays a never-ending game of "Dial-a-Dyke."

There are two women camped nearby. They look to be in their early thirties; wholesome-looking tanned, athletic types. They probably love tennis, eat sushi, and wear white cotton underwear. They drive a blue Honda. I have not seen them away from each other once since they arrived here yesterday morning. They walk together discreetly but closely, they sit in front of their tent in matching lawn chairs listening to their tape deck, they disappear into their tent together as the moon becomes bright and full. I like to suppose that they are on their honeymoon. What if one quiet night I followed the deer path down the hill that separates my campsite from theirs and discovered that they like to leave their tent flap unzipped so they can gaze out at the stars? Brazenly, I'd push the flap all the way back and scurry over to straddle a nearby rock and wait.

Their lithe bodies are backlit by a single lantern. I know they cannot see me hiding in the darkness of the woods outside their tent, but I scrunch down on the rock anyway, trying to make myself smaller. My hardening clit makes contact with a delightful ridge in the smooth saddle-like rock as I lean forward to see and hear what's going on. The maidenly quilted bathrobes and flannel P.J.'s they'd worn to the ladies' room a while ago are now lying in a heap just inside the tent door. My eyes widen like an owl, as I watch. The younger woman straddles her lover's body, positioning her sweet, dripping pussy over the older woman's mouth. I see a long, muscular tongue dart up and down, in and around it, like a hypnotized pink snake. I get a good view of the unfolding lips of the other one's lovenest as her lover leans forward to taste it. She slides both hands under her lover's butt as she pushes the tasty morsel to her searching tongue. At first, their "69" is a lazy exercise in mutual pleasuring. Soon enough, though, the bucking and the moaning begin. They roll convulsively onto their sides, their mouths still magnetized to each other's pussies. First one side of the tent and then the other bulges with the outline of their bodies. Lantern light traces eerie, writhing shadows along the wall. Their flushed bodies are wet with sweat. I find that the rock as well as my jeans are soaked. The aroma of three pussies mingles in the chill night air. They turn out the lantern.

I reluctantly dismount my rock, return to my tent and masturbate myself to sleep.

The next morning, I decide to go for a walk along the lakeshore, in spite of a sky filled with charcoal-colored clouds threatening an imminent downpour. I am halfway around the lake from our tent when the rain starts. Instantly, I am drenched. It is only about 6:00 or 7:00 A.M., and there is no sign of life except for the smell of hot coffee from the convenience store. I have no money, but maybe if they see how wet and bedraggled I am, they'll take pity on me and give me a free cup. I'm so cold; it's worth a try.

The only other person in the store is the cashier. Her dark eyes quickly survey my poor, waterlogged body. As I feel her eyes rivet onto my wet blouse, I notice her emotion change from indifference to, shall we say, compassionate lust. She urges me into the back room so that I can remove my soggy clothing. To allow me greater privacy, she says, she'll lock the front door and put the CLOSED sign in the window for a while. She is almost businesslike as she encases my nakedness in a stadium blanket and efficiently whisks my wet clothes over to the laundromat next door to dry. I surmise from the number of keys she's carrying that she is the person in charge. For all I know, she owns the place.

I'm hopping about on bare feet, clutching the blanket tightly around me with one hand, while I hold the very welcome cup of steaming coffee with the other. I feel her amusedly watching my efforts to get warm. I try to act dumb, but I'm too horny to play games for any length of time. When she finally parts the folds in front of my blanket to slide those warm hands around my waist, I offer no resistance.

Her scarlet fingernails are about an inch long, and she draws them firmly but lightly along my spine, my butt and the backs of my thighs. I shiver from more than the cold. We are about equal in height, but because she has shoes on, at least for now, she's taller than I. She holds my chin in one hand and tips my head back. I feel both my breasts being fondled and squeezed.

She rubs and tugs on my nipples expertly, reawakening them to their attentive state of the night before.

She spreads the blanket on the concrete floor, and we lie down. My belly, inner thighs and clit feel so engorged, I instinctively part my legs. My beautiful hostess decides to breakfast on my tongue. She tastes it and sucks it, running her own tongue round and round it and slurping at it like an ice cream cone. I take matters into my own hands (or legs, in this case) and force her skirt up with my right knee. We fit together like a jigsaw puzzle. It doesn't take me very long to find out she isn't wearing panties. Her clit is as hard as mine as we ride each other's legs. My body is dry enough by now for me to know that the stripe of wetness I leave on her thigh has nothing to do with the rain.

I feel something hard just inside her cunt. I realize she's wearing a tampon, and its string is wedged tightly between her body and my leg. With every movement, friction forces it to move back and forth in her hot, hot pussy. She is crying in Spanish now, "Ai, Dios! Ai, Dios!" over and over. We lie there humping and moaning all tangled up in the checkered blanket for what seems like forever.

We've just started in again for maybe the fourth or fifth time, when we hear someone tapping with a key on the glass front door. My lover jumps up reluctantly to rearrange herself to face her second customer of the morning, but not before she ceremoniously kisses each of my nipples farewell.

I sit there, dazed, sipping the now tepid coffee. I'm listening to her waiting on one customer after another. Then she leaves the store for a few minutes, and soon she's pitching my warm, dry clothes at me along with a blown kiss. It's time to go. Adios, baby.

Fatigue seems to soak into every pore of my being until I feel like I'm made of paper towelling. I practically crawl back to my own tent. Half asleep, I notice a new family has moved into the campsite next to ours. It looks like they're all set up already, and the mom has sent the thunderous herd off for a day of fishing. Some mom! She has prematurely grey hair in a French braid down the middle of her back, she is oh so tan, and she's round in all the right places in her khaki safari shorts and matching midriff shirt.

She's taking a few moments for herself while the dish water

boils, sitting at the picnic table leafing through the stack of vacation books and periodicals. She dreamily sucks her index finger while she gets engrossed in a magazine. Can it be?! It's a woman's erotic magazine! Yes!

I mentally rub my hands together in anticipation. I stick my head and upper body out of the tent flap just far enough so she can see me and wave. "Hi, neighbor!" She looks up with lovely sapphire eyes and focuses on what is not left to the imagination inside my carelessly half-buttoned blouse.

Our families are going to be encouraged to go on a lot of fishing trips this week — and swimming and boating — I can tell.

Jane's Train

Lisa Palac

Coming from the Loop, the Howard was jammed. Jane was lucky to get a seat, even luckier one next to a window. It was one of the old L's, with green and white stickers outlined in red that said *Do Not Stick Head Or Arms Out Of Window*, and who would in late November unless they loved the stench of the underground? The conductor's voice distorted, crackled and clipped off the last syllable of the last word. The train lurched. People fell forward. The lights blinked on, off, then came back on to stay. What would happen if the lights ever stayed out, Jane wondered. Would people get stabbed? Robbed? Maybe raped?

Above ground she rode backwards, watching the street sink below her. Her head against the window, she saw the same things she always saw. Faded Latin Kings graffiti. Ugly turquoise Nova still in the same spot in the junkyard. Back porches peeling grey, loaded down with old refrigerators, kids' bikes, yellowed newspaper, broken glass. The L tracks came so close to the buildings. She imagined what might happen if a train suddenly derailed and smashed right into one of them. Her kitchen window faced west over the tracks and every time a train rolled past the whole building would shake.

"FULLERTON. CHANGE FOR THE RAVENSWOOD. CHANGE FOR THE B TRA —." Jane watched everyone escape. Asian students heading over to De Paul with backpacks and 501s. Wrinkled women wearing babushkas, lugging shopping bags from Jewel. A couple of black guys wearing those white plastic shower caps. Warm mist from everyone's nostrils. Punk rockers in love in matching leather jackets, wasn't that cute? His was falling apart, hers was new just like her messy blonde hair. Red lips, pale face, tons of jewelry on top of black everything and didn't Madonna do that a long time ago? Jane smirked. They smiled. He put his arm around that Blonde waist and squeezed. Perfect lips formed perfect words. The doors slammed. "NO SMOKING OR RADIO PLAYI —." In a frozen second, he saw her dark hair pressed against the glass, those Egyptian eyes. People fell forward. The lights went off.

She opened the door to her apartment, threw her coat on a chair, and lit a cigarette. Usually Jane's random thoughts on the way home from work slipped away as quickly as they came. Not this time. She knew where they were going. To his crummy little place on Walton. To fuck. She loved the thought of it. She had resisted an incredibly childish urge to stick her head and arms out of the train window and scream "FUCK HIM! I DID!" She breathed in the last piece of smoke and put out her cigarette in the tacky ashtray her mother had given her. She watched the glow of the ashes die right on the red heart between I and Chicago.

She flipped on the TV and stretched out on the couch. Her dark hair cut straight across her forehead and then dropped to her shoulders. Eyes outlined in deep blue points did sort of make her look like Cleopatra and she knew it. Queen of Egypt. Satisfied one hundred lovers a night, or so they say. Concentrating on the TV was impossible. The sounds seemed farther and farther away as she slid her hand under her tight red skirt.

They were almost in silhouette, in the kitchen. A red sun melting down the bricks, the glass, dripping onto the tracks outside. Jane could see the shapes of their tongues moving in and out of each other's mouths. The perfect exchange. She liked to start everybody off that way. He circled the Blonde's nipples with his tongue, squeezed them, rubbed them. Jane's hand went to her own breast, under her sweater. Her nipples crinkled up when they got hard.

Fuck the slow removal of clothing, she thought. Go down on the Blonde. Jane wanted to see it. To hear the sounds of licking and sucking and breathing increase. To watch her spread her legs while his tongue drove her crazy. Don't let her come. Tease her. The Blonde pulled him up by the hair to kiss him, to kiss herself. With smooth consistency, she was all over her own mouth, her cheeks. Delicious.

A warm pink flush spread lightly over her chest. The couch was uncomfortable. She got on her knees and made the Blonde do the same. Go ahead. Suck his cock. He brushed the hair away from her face so he could watch. Only traces of red on those lips now, forming perfect O's, again and again, until all of him disappeared. Tell her how beautiful she looks. Tell her how good it feels.

Her fingers had no sensation of their own anymore. They just kept moving faster, soaking wet in tiny circles. All her favorite images repeated themselves. Flashing like a slide show. The words, the things she made them say, she whispered to herself. That familiar sound in the distance wanting her to come. She made them change position until she found one she liked. She wanted them all to come together.

The Blonde felt the cold linoleum on her back, him inside, thumb on her clit. She traced the way the muscles in his arms tensed up. Watching his face and his long hair swing back and forth, imitating their rhythm. Come on. Jane could hear it getting louder now. The vibration spreading out across the floor, up through her body. Fire. The building started to shake. So loud it drowned out all the sound. When the Blonde came. When he came. When the train came. Lasting seconds. Lasting forever.

When she opened her eyes, it was dark. Noise oozing from the idiot box dragged her back to reality. She got up, turned it off, and walked in to the kitchen to get something to eat. The building began to shake, again, but Jane hardly noticed.

Police Protection

Moxie Light

I'd like to be able to say I can smell a hard-on, like hookers and crooks can smell a plainclothesman. But this one was a dead giveaway: macho, from the tip of his curled mustache, down his lean, coiled body to the huge motorcycle buckle on his belt, proclaiming him a "Rider for Justice" on the streets. He was cocky, standing there, proud of his uniform and proud of his badge. As he leaned into the yellow shag of my carpet, thumbs crooked into his belt, inches away from the polished walnut of his gun handle, his fingers unobtrusively caressed the bulging length in his serge.

"What seems to be the problem?" he asked.

I went into my tirade. Child support weeks overdue, robbed, junkies shooting up in the halls, burned-out hulks of cars smoldering on the back streets. Unlike my neighbors, I would never adjust to life in East Boston.

He walked through my living room into the kitchen and opened my refrigerator to see if I was telling the truth. One lonely quart of milk gave witness. The others had been there the night before when I'd reported the robbery. The solid Irish sorts had come that morning, perfunctorily brushing for fingerprints. When this one had come bounding up the stairs, I'd opened the door without a whimper. He introduced himself by his first name — Michael.

"Have you tried welfare?" he asked, with a worried look on his face.

"I don't qualify," I said. My husband was just being spiteful about child support, pressing for a divorce that he'd wanted for years. My five-year-old spent half a day in kindergarten and kept me busy the rest of the time.

"Is there anything I can do for you?"

"My car," I answered. "Please, just don't tow it. I don't have the money to pay for any parking tickets." I didn't really need a car; I never went anywhere. But as soon as I was divorced, I planned to get out of here.

"Here's five dollars," he said. "And my phone number, if you ever need a friend."

I've always hated cops. Sometimes I think I hate cops even more than I hate crooks. I don't like anyone who uses their power for personal advantage. That five dollars made me feel I was selling my soul to the Devil. "I don't want this," I said. "The coffee shop across the street will sport me for breakfast until I can get a loan."

The fiver flew back and forth between us like a feather, until it landed next to a silver-framed picture of a special friend of mine.

"Who's this?" he asked.

Five minutes in my place and this man was delving into my personal life. I didn't like it.

"Please, would you take back the five dollars?" It was humiliating to be this broke.

"Forget it," he said. "I've paid more than that to have someone put their hand on it."

"Out! Out...you wolf in cop's clothing. And if that man..." I pointed to the picture and sputtered, "ever heard you talking to me like that...you...you'd be dead!"

After he left, I worried for weeks about a pervert on the loose. About that sign on me that said I needed a man. The landlord found out I was having trouble paying the rent, and made me the superintendent of the building. After the next robbery, when the next set of cops came, I couldn't keep from asking. "Do you know a Michael? Tall, thin? Vice or narcotics."

"Michael?" They laughed to each other. "You mean, Old Undersheets?"

They were getting to know me at Precinct 7, this hysterical woman on the other end of the phone: seven burglaries, one drunk falling through a first floor window, one overdose and an accidental death, a woman who bled to death while her husband watched television in the next room. Half my tenants were clients at the methadone clinic up the street. As the landlord evicted them, one by one, they blamed me.

I lived in terror, awakened at night by the phone ringing at two, three, and four A.M. with someone who liked to hear my fear-filled voice. My lawyer said that if I moved again before we went to court, the judge would call my home life "unstable," and I would lose custody of my son. I installed a police lock on my door. It had a long iron bar that went into a plate bolted onto the floor, and made a loud grating noise whenever it was used. At six o'clock at night, with all of the locks clunking in my building, it sounded like a lock-up at Alcatraz. Another contraption, of solid steel, was installed in my car, but that didn't keep them from slashing the tires and the convertible top.

Finally, I felt brave enough to press charges for the phone calls. When I walked into the police station, Michael was the cop on the front desk.

"The detectives just went out," he said. "How are things going?" Seeing him made my adrenalin surge.

I began venting my wrath on the zombies at the telephone company who refused to do anything about my late night calls. Michael, with his handlebar mustache, looked like Omar Sharif.

"Do you still have that car with the Florida plates? Do you know you're supposed to re-register after thirty days in this state?"

I gave him a blank look, though I know a veiled threat when I hear one. There had to be a way I could stay on top.

"I'll be over in half an hour," he said. "And we'll see what we can do to make this jungle easier for you."

I went back to my apartment and spent a few minutes putting away my son's playthings. I went into the bathroom to freshen up and run a comb through my damaged hair. My hands trembled as I applied a little makeup and strategic dots of cologne, giving myself a devious wink in the mirror. The victory would be short and sweet. What Michael wanted and what he would get were two different things. For extra bravado, I brought my vibrator out from its hiding place and gave myself a few orgasms, leaning against the bathroom sink.

Michael arrived, and sat on my living room couch, balancing on his knee the cup of coffee that I had ready for him. With his free hand, he patted the couch beside him. His police radio crackled on the coffee table in front of us. "I have to leave it on," he said, apologetically, "in case I get a call."

"All I want to do is survive," I began. "What the hell is going on? Don't you cops ever arrest anybody? One of my tenants, just last week, took off with a refrigerator and stove. The junkie downstairs comes in every night with a different stereo."

"You don't know what it's doing to me," he said, wearily. "When they call us in for the school riots, I have to pop ten Valiums so that some kid doesn't get it between the eyes. The Red Cross even gives us coffee and donuts. Jesus! It was easier overseas."

"Valium?" I hooted. "Even the cops have habits around here. Let me see your arms."

Michael put down his coffee cup and rolled up his sleeves, revealing a thick leather watch band, blue-blooded veins winding snakily up his arm, and several tattoos: Mary, Ann, and Dominique. "I wouldn't know a track if I fell over it," I admitted. "But you sure are one kinky cop with all those tattoos. Are you into S&M?"

"What's that?" he asked, with interest.

"You know, you phony. Whips, chains...."

Michael smiled. "Those tattoos are my sisters' names," he said. "And I can be very gentle. Do you want to try me?" As he rolled down his sleeves, he leaned forward and kissed the bodice of my pinafore. I could feel my nipples straining against the denim.

"Don't you have to be going?" I said, remembering how soft to the touch I had once been. "There are criminals out there on those streets."

"Tell me you don't want me," he said, getting up to draw the drapes. The police radio crackled its garbled jargon. His fingers were at his belt buckle, unzipping his fly. I almost laughed when I saw how ready he was.

"I'm being followed by private detectives," I said, heart pounding, in a last-ditch line of defense.

"All the better," said Michael, as if he knew me better than I did myself. His lips fell soft as rain on mine. His deft fingers rolled my socks down, bringing goose bumps to my knees and tears to my eyes. He was, after all, a public servant and I, when it came down to it, was hungry for affection, if not love. With his foot, Michael pushed the coffee table out of the way. "Tell me you don't want me," he said, enfolding me in his big, strong arms.

"I don't," I whimpered into the hollow of his neck. Then he was kneeling in front of me, with his face in my crotch, blowing short, hot puffs through the silk of my underwear. My hands were on his shoulders, half-pushing him away. One of his fingers inched its way past the elastic on my inner thigh, parting my resistance; his thumb pressed on the tiny, swollen lie.

Tears were pouring down my face as I hid my embarrassment. "I hate you. I hate you," came my muffled cries. Michael pulled me from the couch as if I were a rag doll, all my resistance gone. In one quick motion, he peeled off my underpants and put them on the coffee table next to his revolver. Then he spread my legs and covered me with his body, still fully dressed, kissing my tears and whispering passionately in my ears.

All the while he pressed himself rhythmically into the gnawing ache of my groin. Soon, a wonderful warm wave began radiating through my whole body. An involuntary moan came from my throat as all the pent-up pressures and loneliness began to recede. My hands fell limp by my sides and Michael undressed me.

It was as if I were hypnotized. His fingertips tracing the curves of my body...his touch both electric and sensual...my hips rolling in an unforgettable motion of their own...my breath coming hard and fast as he bent his head to my quivering thighs, licking, licking, with soft little animal sounds, bringing me to a peak of sensation. It was more than I could handle. My mind felt as if it were unhinging, reeling into a starless void.

"Please, please...." I was afraid and the pleasure had turned to pain. I struggled to free myself from his grip, suddenly sitting up, hands flying, not knowing what to cover first.

"Shhh!" said Michael, kissing my eyelids, one at a time. "Let me. You don't have to do anything but enjoy."

"It hurts," I said, not being able to explain, not even under-standing myself how this whole thing had come about. I had never made love to a stranger before.

"You're dry," said Michael, reaching for his handcuffs. "You're shy and I have just the cure." Firmly, with his other hand, he pushed me down, at the same time running the tip of his tongue around one of my nipples, sucking so gently that it made me weak with desire. I shut my eyes as Michael un-dressed. The air was thick with the smell of lust. He cuffed my wrists to the couch.

This time, instead of the tip of his tongue, Michael used his hands, kneading me between the legs, his knowing fingers bringing me to a passion I'd never known, not all my married life. I could feel the faint prick of his whiskers on my swollen lips as he lifted my buttocks to his mouth; heard the sound of his full tongue, over and over, as I became wet. Then he did something with his nightstick which drove me absolutely crazy, moving it in and out, flicking the tip of my clit with his tongue, massaging my breasts, my buttocks, everywhere at once, it seemed, until I begged him to stop. As I struggled against my bonds and squirmed against the long, hard strokes, my whole body broke out in a sweat, so that I could feel the spray flying as I tossed my head from side to side, fighting the powerful force.

"Do you want me yet?" asked Michael, smiling from the heights.

"Untie me, you sadist," I managed to gasp, just before he did exactly that. And with a great deal of thrashing, sweaty-limbed and all, forgetting all propriety, I climbed over Michael and rode him on waves of ecstasy, over and over, up and down, slowing down every time I felt him ready to explode, then starting up again.

"Mercy," cried Michael, reaching to pull me down to him and entwine our tongues. Now it was me, stretched out full length on him, reaching for his toes with my own, circling his penis with a tightening grip, rotating slowly, coaxing him to come. Michael's fingers pulled on my hair, signalling me, as if we'd been partners for years, until a final, surrealistic shudder passed through our bodies. The feeling lingered for a few joyful seconds. I was flooded with a sense of power.

Sex Education

Jesse Linnell

I pulled up to the driveway, turned off the engine and sat, reluctant to move. Except for the porch light and a light upstairs, the house at the end of the drive was dark. I was glad no one had waited up for me.

The house belonged to Rob and Jenna, a couple I knew only slightly. My old friend Beth had talked me into coming down here for the weekend, promising a great time at the beach. A few days ago, I had broken up with my lover of two years, and though I was glad of the decision, the loss of Everett made me want to retreat into myself. For a moment, I was tempted to turn around and head home. They would never know I'd been here. I could call tomorrow with some excuse.

However, I never did such things, so I got my bag out of the trunk and walked up to the house.

The key was under a flower pot, as Jenna had said it would be, along with a note from Beth telling me my bedroom was the first at the top of the stairs. She'd added at the botom: "Glad you made it. It'll be a good weekend." I smiled at the reassuring words.

I opened the door and walked quietly across the dimly lit living room, past Beth and her lover, Kevin, who were asleep on a fold-out couch. Their sleeping faces sent a pang through me. It was hard to look at lovers.

My bedroom was warm and close from the heat of the day. From across the hall came the faint thumping bass of a rock song. Someone was awake, but I didn't feel like investigating. I changed into pajamas and opened the window wide. Below me was the back yard. A high fence sheltered a small patio, a strip of lawn and a swimming pool. I stared at an odd, black lump at the side of the pool, and decided it was an inner tube. I hadn't seen an inner tube in ten years, I thought. There was a tap at the door, and it swung open.

"Is the radio too loud?"

I looked up at a slightly built, barefoot young man, wearing a T-shirt and jeans. I guessed he was around seventeen.

"No, it's okay," I said.

We introduced ourselves.

He was Chris, Jenna's cousin. He'd been spending the summer with Rob and Jenna while working at the Marine Center. He wanted to be an oceanographer. This fall he was starting college in California. "Ever been out there?" he asked.

I shook my head.

"The coast is incredible. Want to see some pictures I took last year?"

"Sure." We moved to his room.

We sat on his bed and he handed me photos of hulking brown sea lions, draped across rocks in the sun; a brown blur he said was a pelican; the sheer side of a cliff, where he pointed out the remains of cormorants' nests. His voice was high-pitched with eagerness. I thought of Everett, who dismissed so many books, places and people as "a goddamn waste of time." Chris' curly hair was deep brown, almost black, and his skin a light golden-brown. His fingers brushed mine as he handed me the pictures. For a moment I was aware of my breasts under the thin pajamas, but I quickly flicked the thought away. Sexual feelings and men his age were in separate corners of my mind.

We talked about California and animals and then about college. He was surprised to hear that I was an instructor at the university, and he asked about the classes I taught, and what I thought of my students. At two o'clock, we said good night, and I walked back to my room, smiling. What a nice kid, I thought.

The next morning, the whole household packed into Jenna's car and drove off to the beach. We trudged over sand dunes with bags of food, a cooler, blankets and towels, and came upon a perfect beach scene: bright umbrellas, motionless sunbathers glistening with sweat and lotions, radios blaring against the sound of the blue-green water lapping at the shore. We unfurled towels and pulled off T-shirts and shoes. I plopped down on a blanket with my detective novel.

A few feet away, Chris was climbing out of his jeans. His legs were tapered like a colt's. His chest was broad. A few dark hairs curled up his belly from the waistband of his suit. I looked down quickly at my book.

"Aren't you coming in?" Chris asked.

"I don't like swimming in the ocean," I said apologetically. "I'm always wondering what's down in the water that I can't see."

He hesitated. "Well, I guess I'll go in without you, then."

He ran down to the water with long, easy strides. He ran through the waves and, as a curl of water surged to meet him, he dived under it. I watched the water, looking for him. At last he bobbed up between waves, and began to swim in smooth strokes.

I turned back to my book. The detective couldn't decide what time the murder had taken place.

Chris was floating on his back just beyond where the waves were breaking, the ocean slowly rocking him.

The heat made me feel listless. I lay back and closed my eyes, half listening to the sound of the waves and a barking dog. A panting sound came closer and closer. It was Chris, running in from the water. He reached our spread of blankets, grabbed a towel, and began rubbing his face. His chest was heaving, dripping; his dark brown nipples taut and wet. I could see the bulge of his penis under his wet suit. A hot flush spread across my chest.

"Water's nice and warm," he gasped. "You should try it."

"No thanks," I said.

He lay down on his towel, his smooth brown back moving slightly as his breathing calmed. Drops of water, iridescent in the sun, hung on his curls. I wanted to scatter them with my hand. Instead, I jerked myself upright.

"I'm going for a walk," I said. "See you later."

I walked off down the beach, my blood pounding. The year I had first lived with a man, this Chris was probably learning to ride a tricycle. I had never been excited by a man this young. And I couldn't imagine him being excited by me. When I was his age, I had never desired anyone older. I decided that neither Chris nor anyone else would learn of my attraction.

But all afternoon, my body told me of his presence. He sat next to me on the trip home. The shoulder that touched his, the arm and thigh and knee that were next to him knew his every move. At dinner, I watched his full lips as he talked, and my own parted expectantly. As I rose to go to bed, I felt a wetness between my legs.

Chris caught up with me on my way up the stairs. "Want to go for a drive or something?" he said.

He looked so friendly and open — and so young. I felt so deceitful and messy, with my hidden thoughts and sticky crotch. I couldn't believe he was offering what my body wanted.

"I don't think so, Chris," I said. "I'm pretty tired."

"Guess it is kind of late," he said. "See you tomorrrow."

"Good night."

I closed the door to my room and felt like crying. I got into bed with my detective novel. I didn't want to think about Chris, or anything else.

I read, wishing the story would speed up. The detective still hadn't figured out when the damn murder had taken place. I kept squirming under the sheet, my body warm and restless. Finally, I sighed, turned out the light and began stroking a familiar path between my thighs. I let my fingers drift upward across my stomach and up my chest. My fingertips teased my nipples, caressing them to stiffness.

I opened my eyes to see the light from his room framing my door. Then I shut them and let my hand begin to comb through a tangle of pubic hair. My mind roamed swiftly through a catalog of fantasies, selecting The Ravishment.

The fingers became a probing tongue. Hot breath surrounded it, sending a fire through my thicket of hair. A hand reached from behind me to play endlessly with my breasts. Another greedy tongue stroked and sucked and pushed my own. The image of Chris's face intruded, his lashes blackly wet, as he bent over a towel. A penis rubbed against my ass, throbbing at the feel of my skin. A woman's nipples, teasingly erect, nuzzled mine. The tongue at my vulva probed one side of my clit. I imagined Chris at the doorway, watching my ravishment hungrily, his jeans bulging with an enormous erection.

A satiny penis glided inside me and began moving up and down. A hard clit pressed against my thigh, leaving a wet trail. The tongue played with my clit relentlessly; nothing would stop it. My thoughts called out silently: *I want you, Chris. Want you.* The penis slid faster in and out.

I started to come.

"Ah."

My head moved from side to side. My clit and vagina were joined in one burning path. *Want you, Chris. Please.*

"Ahhh."

I didn't care if he heard me. *Fuck me, Chris!*

"AHHHHH!"

My body jerked and my vagina clutched my finger in spasms. I wound down, moving my finger until I was quiet inside. Around me, the house was silent. The light under his door had gone out. I lay in stillness, wondering if he'd heard me. I hoped he had. I wanted him to know.

I drifted off with the image of his full lips hovering close to mine.

Sunday morning, everyone gathered for breakfast. It was assumed we would spend another day at the beach, but I said I wanted to laze around the pool. Beth looked at me sympathetically, probably assuming I wanted some time alone to mourn the loss of Everett. But I was thinking of Chris. I didn't want to spend another day at the beach helplessly staring at him. I hoped crazily that he would stay behind, too. I felt idiotic, passively waiting for a sign from him. But I was unsteady on this new ground, afraid to pursue him openly as I would an older man.

Chris announced he'd skip the beach. He had some things to do around the house. I wondered what they were.

After the others had left, I put on my suit, got my towel and detective novel, and walked out to the lawn. The sun reflected off the pool, turning the water bright turquoise and making me squint. I settled down in the stretch of shade along the fence. The lawn was covered with tiny green flowerettes that had fallen from the trees overhead.

I began reading, and found that the detective had finally pinpointed the time of the murder. Well, that was something. I looked up at Chris's window, wondering if he was still in his room. I decided that if I didn't see him soon, I'd go inside and start a conversation. I had no idea what I'd say.

The screen door banged and Chris walked out in his swimsuit, towel in hand.

"Thought I'd give you some company," he said. He wasn't looking at me.

"Be my guest," I said.

He unrolled his towel and lay down next to me. "Nice out here," he said.

"Yeah." It was an effort to speak. The long slope from the rise of his shoulder to the small of his back was so beautifully curved, so softly golden-brown it made my throat ache.

He noticed my book, where a sprinkling of flowerettes had settled. "These things get all over the place," he said. He leaned over and brushed them off the page.

He wants to touch me, I thought. But I lay as if frozen. For a brief, horrid moment, I imagined him saying to friends: "This older woman came on to me. It was weird." I drove the image away. I couldn't face going back home tomorrow, never knowing if he wanted me at all. I had to try.

"You've got some on you already," I said. I brushed a few flowerettes from his shoulders. Then my hand stroked slowly down his back.

He lay unmoving for a moment. Then, in one quick movement, his arm circled my back and drew me to him. In a huge release, I pressed my mouth to his.

He wanted me. I was light-headed, delighted. Our kissing and hugging became so prolonged that I realized this might be all he expected from our coming together. But his desire had made me bold. I took off the top of my suit and was instantly gratified as his mouth and hands traveled over my breasts as if he couldn't touch them, taste them enough. I felt voluptuous, irresistible. I pulled at his suit; he yanked it down over his legs and kicked it away. I wanted to look at him but his chest was across mine.

I felt the intensity fading from his arms and lips. I knew what had happened even before he said, "It's gone soft."

I kissed him on the mouth. "That doesn't matter," I said. "It feels good just to touch."

I pulled off my swimsuit bottom as he watched, and lay alongside him. I caressed his neck and shoulders, and cupped my hand over the slight swell of his belly, which was downy on the surface and taut within. I played my fingers under the soft bundle of balls and penis, loving the roundness and weight of them.

He pulled me tight to him and our kisses became faster. A movement against my belly — his penis jerking as it swelled erect — made me gasp.

I pushed one leg over his thigh. "Touch me with it," I whispered.

"Like this?" The mushroom head pressed against my clit.

"Like this." I rubbed lightly against him.

He took over. The friction was unbearably sweet. I imagined the cleft of his penis head as it moved against my stiff, rosy clit. Then the tip of his penis was just inside me. *Yes.* I pushed forward onto it. He rolled on top of me, and thrust deep inside, plunging and pumping. I held on to his shoulders. A pulsing started in my vagina, ran through my body, then outside me, becoming rhythmic cries. Chris stopped mid-plunge, groaned, and sank on top of me.

We held each other, stroking and kissing. He faced me then, smiling. He was loose and warm and exhilarated.

"Was this your first time?" I asked.

"First time it was any good," he said, laughing. "Let's go in."

"Inside?"

"In the *water.* Come on."

The cool water was a delightful shock. I hadn't been swimming without a suit in years and was surprised all over again how light and free my body felt. I churned through the water, huffing, in a determined effort at a crawl. Chris skimmed by me underwater, a slim sea creature. The light dappled over him. He reached the end of the pool, flipped into a smooth somersault and shot out toward me. All at once he rose up beneath me, his chest under mine, his arms loosely around me.

"Turn over," he said.

I turned over on my back and he pulled me gently up his

chest. My head was on his shoulder, his hand beneath my breasts. I stiffened, and strained to hold my head well out of the water.

"Just float," he said. "I'll hold you up."

He pulled me along effortlessly, hardly stirring the water. Finally, I relaxed into the rhythmic surge of his body. I let myself go limp; my legs trailed behind me.

We reached the shallow water, where he lifted me into the half-inflated inner tube and kissed me.

"Show me what you were doing last night," he said.

I stared up at him. He'd heard.

"Show me. I want to do it to you."

I hesitated, then opened my legs over the swell of the inner tube, and began to stroke the side of my clit. My face became quickly hot. I was self-conscious but excited. I'd never shown this to anyone.

He leaned close to watch, bringing up dripping fingers to tease my nipples. Then he gently pushed my hand away and began to finger my clit. His mouth bent to mine. His wet lips looked almost red. I sucked his tongue. His black curls glistened. His mouth, hot, wet, traveled my neck, my shoulder, and fastened on my nipple, kissing, sucking, making it melt.

I closed my eyes. The heat beat down on us. The inner tube, cradling my steaming body, bobbed slightly up and down. Chris pushed down on the front of the tube, and water lapped up, just covering my pubic hair. His fingers parted my labia, his mouth dipped into the water, and he blew a torrent of bubbles which tickled over my vulva. Then, his mouth still underwater, he lapped his tongue at my clit. I began to whimper and pant. I wanted him inside me. "Let's get out," I said, my voice thick with urgency.

We scrambled out of the pool and raced to our towels. His penis, erect in a glorious curve, bounced stiffly as he ran. We fell onto the towels and I rolled on top and sat astride his thighs. I grasped his swollen penis and put it just inside me so he could feel how wet I was, how much I wanted him. His eyes were closed; he looked sweetly asleep, except that his lips were parted in a way that made my blood beat hot in my vulva. I eased myself slowly onto his engorged penis. I reached behind and clutched his balls. He moaned.

I began to move up and down. He rose into me, his breath

coming hard. The sensation was sweet, sweeter. My insides, so thick and tight with desire, uncurled. I came in long shudders. Chris went rigid and a cry came from deep within him. I lay down on him and held him fast.

We lay there, wet from sweat and sex and water from the pool. I was lazily content, my face buried in his warm curls. But Chris was energized. He wanted to go in again.

He pulled me upright and led me across the grass to the edge of the pool. The concrete burned pleasantly at our feet. He turned to me with an excited grin.

"Climb on my back," he said. "We'll dive in together."

"Oh, no, Chris." I drew back. All at once I felt brittle and old.

"It's okay," he said. "I won't let you fall." His eyes were dancing. His warm fingers tightened on mine.

"You're crazy," I said, half laughing.

He could tell I'd softened. "You get on my shoulders," he said, "and I'll stand up. Then you stand up and we'll dive in."

He squatted down and I sat on his shoulders, my wet pubic hair against his neck. He gripped my hands, and slowly rose.

"Now stand up," he said.

Awkwardly, I brought one foot up on his shoulder. The glittery concrete looked far away. "Jesus, Chris, I don't know," I said.

"It's okay, I've got you."

I brought my other foot to his shoulder as I hoisted myself jerkily upright. I stood, my bent knees wobbling, my hands clamped to his. His body held me firm.

"Now!" he said.

He lunged forward. I pushed off his shoulders. The sheet of blue rushed toward me. The impact and splash, the surge of water and bubbles thrilled me. I bobbed up to the surface, laughing and hiccuping. I had done it.

My young lover surfaced, smiling as he saw my face. We swam to the side and kissed. He ran his hand up the side of my neck, under my hair.

"Tonight I'll take you swimming in the ocean," he said. "You'll love it."

I believed him.

Workout

Khasti Cadell

No one could have been more bushed than I was. The tension in my muscles seemed to have worked its way into my bones. All week long I had been working hard, and now my body needed to relax.

I called Zora, my buddy who belongs to a trendy health club in Flatbush. The locker room there is a study hall for the appreciation of the body. This is more than your ordinary sweat club.

Zora was trying to get herself into a health club regimen, and she had asked me several times to join her at the club for swimming, sauna, steam room, and massage. She was delighted that I agreed to go with her this afternoon.

I packed my big blue towel, my bathing suit and some skin creams into a small duffle bag and rushed out to the subway so I could meet her by four o'clock.

When I arrived, only a few women were in the club. It was a little early for the after-work crowd. Just as well, for it gave me a chance to have some privacy with Zora.

I love Zora's body. Although we're buddies, not lovers, we

had made love a few times when one of us needed the other. You could say we are friends in love. Besides, she has the most beautifully soft, smooth chocolate skin.

I stripped off my clothes in front of the lockers in the ell off the main area. Zora stood there already naked, her beautiful brown breasts inviting me to kiss them. I pulled her to me and took her nipple in my mouth, feeling it grow as hard and round as a pearl as I sucked it gently.

"Hey, Khasti, I thought you came here for a little relaxation, baby," Zora said, grinning. But she didn't pull away. She stroked my shoulders and my back as she nuzzled my hair.

"I did. But I thought I should give the hostess appropriate thanks." I concentrated on her other nipple, holding her tit from underneath, lifting it to my mouth.

We leaned up against the lockers. Zora touched my cunt lightly with her fingertips, teasing her hand between my thighs and back toward my asshole. I groaned softly. She knew what I liked. I felt fingers entering my cunt, two, then three. I like to feel full in there. She pressed my clit with her thumb.

"How're you feeling now, Khasti, huh? Are you relaxing yet?"

"I'm starting to, uh, unwind...." I kissed her deeply in her mouth. Her tongue played with mine. "Let's move over to where we can be more comfortable, okay?"

We took my big blue towel and laid it on the floor next to the side of the bank of lockers. Zora nuzzled my ear and neck and stroked my thigh.

I couldn't help it. My legs opened to her stroke, and she put her fingers back into my cunt, which was by now dripping and swollen. But I wanted something else as well.

"Zora, I've got to eat you. Open up." I shifted her legs apart, and she bent her knees. I knelt between her legs and she lay back. Her clit was hard and already straining out of the hood. I sucked it gently first, then harder. I fingered her while I sucked. I knew that she loved that, to feel me inside her cunt and sucking her clit hard. Her sweet juice began to flow over my lips, my chin.

"Turn," she whispered. "Turn. Let me have you too."

I positioned my cunt right over her mouth. I felt her straining to reach me and heard her sigh with contentment when she could bite my clit. Her tongue was running all over my pussy, and she stuck it into me as deep as she could. Her mouth returned and she sucked my clit hard, biting with her teeth and shoving her fingers deep inside me. Zora always knew exactly what I wanted as if it were second nature. Her other hand busied herself on my nipple, squeezing hard, rolling it around between her fingers.

I felt the explosion begin. There is always a moment when you know there is no return. You can't stop it by concentrating on your partner's pleasure, you can't stop it by thinking of baseball scores or her tits or her legs wrapped around you lovingly. All you can think of is coming yourself. Zora was getting me there, and she insisted on triumph.

I came, showering her face with my juice. Her cunt was straining toward me, and I sucked it until she came in my mouth, soaking my face and my fingers.

"Are you feeling better now?" she asked.

We sat up against the lockers again, our arms around each other. We both felt good, and finally ready to join the rest of the world.

"Hey, you dykes finished?"

We looked up. The locker room attendant was standing over us. She was about 5'11" and must have weighed 275. She wore a light blue shirt and dark blue slacks. I opened my eyes a little wider.

"You know, this happens to be a public place. We can't have people sucking and fucking wherever they want. Zora, you're a member here, and you should know better. You better come with me, both a'you."

"Don't worry," Zora whispered to me. "Ruth just wants a piece of the action. She probably saw your ass and wants to fuck it."

I smiled to myself, and felt my asshole begin to react with pleasure.

Ruth escorted us to her office, a small room with a desk and a chair and a shade on the door's window.

"There's nothing I hate more than a coupla dykes tryin' to take advantage of the hospitality here at the club." The message was tough, but she had a strange softness in her voice. "I'm gonna have to teach ya a lesson. Now you, Zora, you know better, so I can only think that this bitch here forced you to forget the rules. Is that it?"

"Yes, ma'am," answered Zora meekly.

"Well, bitch, you don't want to be able to come back here, is that it?"

"No, ma'am," I said, taking my cue from Zora.

"Well, then, I can see you're gonna need to be punished for disobeying the rules. And Ruth is gonna do the punishing."

"Yes, ma'am."

She looked beyond me to the window with the shade pulled almost all the way down. "I always leave the shade up a little so if any of the other girls get the same idea you dykes had, they can see what happens."

She unzipped her pants. "Now turn over on that desk. I don't wanna hear a peep from you. Zora, you just stand and watch me fuck your little girl friend here. Don't you move."

Ruth pushed me down so that I was leaning over, with my face resting on the cool wood of the desk. She searched through a desk drawer to collect what she needed. Suddenly she was behind me, fingering my cunt.

"Nice and wet in there." She moved her hand to my ass, kneading and massaging her way toward my asshole. She started to touch me lightly around the edge. My muscles tightened and my ass lifted in anticipation.

"Oh, this ain't nuthin' new to you, is it? I'll bet you like a little ass fucking now and then, don't you?"

"Yes, ma'am," I said softly.

She stopped, and I heard her pants drop to the floor. I waited a moment. "Turn around, bitch. I want you to suck this thing, bitch, and I want you to suck it good."

Kneeling in front of her, I opened my mouth to take in her dildo. She shoved it deep into my mouth. I felt my cunt get wetter, hotter. I put my hands around her ass to pull her closer. Suddenly she pulled out.

"Back up on the desk, bitch. I wanna fuck that ass of yours."

I turned around and assumed the position she had originally placed me in.

"You better be ready, bitch," I heard her mutter, and I felt something cold and creamy being rubbed onto my asshole. I felt the big dildo at the entrance to my ass. She began to push it in. I smiled. This is what I had been waiting for, this is what I loved. I felt her fill up my ass with it, pushing in and pulling out with a hard rhythm. Ruth moved her fingers onto my clit and pulled me closer to her. I wished she would fuck me forever. Suddenly I felt the familiar beginnings of an orgasmic explosion. I began to breathe louder.

"Shut up. I don't wanna hear you come, bitch. I just wanna feel it."

I closed my eyes, quieted my still deep and ragged breath, and rocked to the rhythm. I started to sweat. Everything broke apart, and I never wanted to leave the heaven I was in.

"Had enough?"

"Yes, ma'am." She pulled the dildo out of my ass slowly. Then she shoved it back in, deep and hard.

"Just remember this when you decide to go public in my locker room again." She turned to Zora, who had been watching with her fingers up her cunt and was now leaning against the wall. "And listen, missy, next time you bring a guest to the club, remind her of the rules. Otherwise...." Ruth mock-glared at Zora, who was standing with her head coquettishly bowed.

She turned back to me. "Bitch, you got a name?"

"Yes, ma'am." I looked her in the eye and smiled. "Khasti."

"Well, Khasti, you keep acting cute like that, and I'll have to come down hard on you whenever you're here. You want that?"

"Yes, ma'am."

Ruth smiled. "Well, good. Then we have an understanding, don't we? You and Ruth know exactly where we stand, don't we?"

"Yes, ma'am. I know *exactly* where to stand. And how, too."

"You dykes are dismissed."

Zora and I walked out and closed the door behind us. We looked up, and we saw three or four other women standing nearby smiling at us. They'd watched Ruth fuck me!

"Yo, how was it?" "Did you like it?" "Isn't she great?" They clapped me on the back, slapped me on my ass. "Ruth must have liked you!"

Affairs

Charmaine Parsons

Doris reached for the meat on the top rack and caught her reflection in the freezer's metal plating. As her blouse rode up it revealed the roll of loose flesh at her hips. She quickly stuck the package in her shopping cart and pulled her top over the flaw. There was a smudge on the hem of her blouse. The day was hot and she could feel her hair straggling from the ponytail and clinging limply around her face. Her makeup felt greasy. A young man reached past her for a package of hamburger. He smiled and she drew herself up and smiled back. She finished her grocery shopping in a better frame of mind.

The check-out boy was short but muscular. He was confident and aware of his physical magnetism. He moved with the fluid grace of the young and the good looking. Doris stole appraising glances as her purchases were tallied. She flushed slightly when he picked up the box of douche preparation, but he tucked it into the bag as casually as if it were a loaf of bread.

She fumbled her change paying for her purchases. He scooped up the quarter and handed it back to her. He didn't smile or even look at her. But she was sure his hand hovered a little longer than necessary; there was a lingering contact between their flesh. She tingled pleasantly, then told herself it was just her imagination.

After the cool of the store, the hot afternoon air hit like a blast furnace. Doris began to wilt. She led the boy with her groceries to the car. Unconsciously she put an extra wiggle into her hips.

The young man loaded the groceries quickly and shut the trunk lid with a bang.

"There you go," he announced in a bored monotone.

She held out a quarter tip and as he took it, their eyes met. An electric charge passed between them. She caught her breath but could tell he had felt the same. He took the quarter and his eyelids lowered sleepily.

"I get off in ten minutes," he whispered. "I have a car — a van — in the back lot." He gathered up a few loose carts and then looked over his shoulder. "Meet me."

She opened her mouth to protest, but he was already halfway back to the store. She climbed into her car slowly. She couldn't meet him. She was a married woman. She started up the car and drove off toward the back of the store.

Doris traced his bare chest with her forefinger. "I have to be going soon," she said softly.

He nodded and took another drag on the cigarette. She watched his handsome young face in profile. Probably some Latin blood someplace, she decided.

"I shouldn't have done this," she said.

This time he turned his head to look at her. "A woman like you shouldn't belong to just one man."

"I won't be able to see you again."

He merely nodded and looked away....

It was over. It had been good but now it was over. She got up and began to dress.

She put the bag of groceries on the kitchen table and peered into the living room. Her husband was slumped in the easy chair, stocking feet on the hassock and a can of beer in one hand. There was a ball game blaring and the room had the aroma of malt liquor and stale feet.

"I'm home," Doris called.

Bert didn't look up from the ball game. She shrugged and

began putting away the groceries. She hadn't expected a response.

Bert shuffled into the kitchen as she was preparing dinner. She heard fast jangling music from the TV and a voice proclaiming the good movie to come so she knew the game was over.

Bert lifted the lid from one of the bubbling pots and squinted at the contents. "What's for dinner?" he asked.

Doris began setting the table. "Pork chops, potatoes, bread, peas...."

Bert bobbed his head, which was as close as he ever came to expressing approval. "I'm starved."

"Be ready in a minute. Go wash up." She looked him over. "Why don't you change shirts?"

He peered down in puzzlement and plucked at the shirt he was wearing. "What's wrong with this?"

She shook her head sadly. "It's full of holes. And you need a shave."

He chuckled and leaned over to rub his coarse cheek against her neck. "My shirt's fine and you love me rough and rugged."

She pushed him away playfully and coyly lowered her head. "Go on now. Get washed up."

Bert ate dinner with gusto, leaning back at the conclusion and punctuating it with a large belch.

"Bert!" Doris admonished.

"Got that job to do tomorrow," Bert said. "Guess I'd better hit the sack." He paused suggestively. "You coming?"

It was his standard invitation to sex. Doris nodded. "Let me get a few things cleaned up and I'll be in. I have to see Dr. Cheeves tomorrow, so I'll shower in the morning."

Doris ruffled through her magazine with a definite lack of interest. She felt small beads of perspiration on her upper lip and licked at them nervously. She wondered if any woman ever felt comfortable going to a gynecologist.

When it was her turn the nurse weighed her, charted and assessed her complaints and then filed her away in a small cubicle with instructions to go to Room Two when she was "ready."

She undressed quickly, folding her clothes neatly on the little bench with her underwear and bra concealed. The paper gown was flimsy protection. She slipped into it carefully so it wouldn't tear. She slid back the door, peered out and scurried to the designated area. Only when she had shut the door and draped the cloth sheet over her lap was she able to relax.

The doctor shuffled in slowly. There were tired purple circles under his eyes, but he greeted Doris warmly.

"Got that infection again, huh?" he asked, scanning her chart.

She nodded miserably.

"Weight's up a few pounds," he admonished. "Better get it off. The older you are the harder it gets."

She made a false promise to do something about it.

He had her lie back and put her feet in the stirrups. She flinched as he pulled up the sheet to expose her and clicked on the hot bright lamp. He settled himself below her field of vision. He confirmed his suspicions and withdrew his instrument. The back of his hand brushed against the inside of her thigh and it seemed to her he prolonged that contact.

He rose and did a quick physical exam. "I'll write you a prescription," he said. She still lay with her feet in the stirrups, too shy to put her legs together until told.

"You can get dressed now," he said, moving toward the door.

She closed her eyes and heaved a sigh of relief that the ordeal was over. She began to move from her awkward position when suddenly the doctor was back at her feet.

"What's the matter?" she asked, raising herself from the table, too stunned to realize her legs were still in the spread position.

He leaned over her, pressing the length of his body between her legs and forcing her shoulders back on the table.

"Doris, please," he whispered hoarsely, "I know this is all wrong. I know I shouldn't behave this way with a patient, and I pray to God you won't turn me in, but, Doris...." His voice caught in his throat and he pushed himself back to a standing position. "You are so special, and I've wanted you for so long." He lifted the sheet and looked down at her with moist eyes. "You're so beautiful." He raised his eyes to her face. "Please let me make love to you," he begged.

She knew it was wrong, but the raw lust in his eyes was more than she could bear. She held out her arms to him. "Yes...Jim. It's all right."

And because he was a doctor and knew all of a woman's secret places, it was wonderful — absolutely wonderful.

While she waited for Bert to come home, Doris started dinner cooking and scrubbed the bathroom. She refrained from gagging as she cleaned Bert's hair from the bathtub drain. The man was a gorilla.

"What did the doctor tell you?" Bert asked that night around a mouthful of steak.

She lifted her shoulders with a shrug. "Got that infection again," she said sadly.

"Jesus!" Bert snorted. "Does that mean I have to take those crappy pills again to keep from passing it back?" She nodded. "Jesus," he muttered again.

Bert began raving about "the stupid way women are put together" but she concentrated on her dinner and tuned him out.

They spent the rest of the day as they did every Wednesday evening. They watched a new crime drama featuring the old combination of two young radical cops. There was the predictable blond who was like a brother to his equally adorable brown-haired male friend. They were rude without being abrasive, good looking, tanned, with wide shoulders and tight little backsides. Doris would never admit it, but she enjoyed the show as much as Bert, but for a different reason.

Tonight, though, she was bored and restless. Halfway through the show she decided to leave the two detectives, Stan and Jim, arguing over police procedure. She had just lowered herself into the bathtub and begun to relax when the door opened. Stan, the blond cop, shut the door behind him and eyed her body hungrily through the murky bath water.

"Jim couldn't make it tonight," he said, "but we both have a real treat for you next week."

He began to undress. Doris resettled in the tub and smiled happily.

Our Friends Fran and Jan

Susan St. Aubin

When I tell people about Fran and Jan, they think I'm talking about two women, or that Jan is the man and Fran is the woman. Actually, their names are Francis and Janine, and they've been together for twenty-three years, ever since they ran away to New Orleans to get married when they were seventeen. They were Ed's friends first. He used to be a free-lance paralegal until Fran hired him part-time and encouraged him to start law school. That was two years ago, when Ed and I began living together. I even worked in Fran's law office for a while as a receptionist, but I couldn't stand it. Now I work with computers for a bank, which I like better because I don't have to talk to anyone.

Fran and Jan have this great old house he inherited, along with a lot of money, when his mother's aunt died ten years ago. It's three stories, with three bedrooms on the third floor, a library and a sitting room on the second floor, and a kitchen and dining room on the ground floor. There's also an attic with two guest rooms that have the best views in the house.

Jan was born in New Orleans and likes to say she's a mulatto though she's no darker than I am, with straight brown hair and a small pointed nose. Fran met her in Dallas where they both went to high school. He was born in San Francisco, but his father was a city planner who moved all over the country. Jan was a model for a while in New York, and made enough money to put Fran through school, which was a good thing, because for the first few years they were married his family wouldn't give him a cent.

Jan always looks like she's posing in front of lights and a camera, even though she doesn't model any more, except for an occasional department store ad for the Sunday paper, where she's always identified as "Jan Rose, wife of well-known defense lawyer Francis Rose, photographed in the library of their Victorian home."

One warm Friday night a couple of months ago, Ed and I and Roger and John, two of Jan's friends from Hollywood, were sitting around the oak table in the Roses' dining room after dinner. We were talking about the history of the house. Jan sat with her best profile to us, looking off in the distance beyond Fran's head. She took a sip of wine and licked her bottom lip.

"It was built before the Civil War," she said. "The original owners used to hide runaway slaves in the basement."

"By the time they got here they didn't need to hide," said Fran. "They could work in the gold mines like everyone else. But that's irrelevant because this house was built in the 1890s, long after the Civil War. I've seen the records — you can look up the complete history of your house, when it was built, when it was sold."

Jan picked up her wine glass, curling her little finger around the stem. "An architect told me it must have been built around 1848."

"He didn't have the facts," said Fran. "1890."

"Facts," said Jan, "aren't everything." She smiled at me as if we were conspirators, or could be. I was confused; usually, she ignored me.

While Fran glowered at his empty plate, Ed patted Jan on the head and murmured, "Don't worry, I believe you no matter what Fran's facts are." Then he asked Fran, "Have you ever explored your basement? My uncle found a box of old campaign buttons in his basement in Berkeley. 'Win with Wilkie,' that kind of thing."

"There's nothing there," Fran answered. "And no light to see it by. No windows, either. My Aunt Ginnie used to stand at the top of the stairs and pitch stuff she didn't want down there — dresses, empty boxes, old magazines. It's a trash pit."

"But Ed's right," said Jan. "We should have a look around." She held Ed's hand in her lap.

To tell the truth, I was always uncomfortable at Fran and Jan's house. I knew Ed had had an affair with Jan before he moved in with me, and I knew they were still seeing each other. I couldn't put my suspicion into words, not even to myself, and Ed didn't talk about it. There was a lot unspoken between us.

I didn't like the way Fran corrected everything Jan said, either, or the way he glared at her from behind his bushy beard. But then he always seemed to glare; his heavy black eyebrows knit together in a frown even when he laughed. Now he scowled at Ed, saying, "We should preserve the basement as it is." He filled his glass from the carafe on the table and raised it. "To the unknown forces at the bottom," he said with his frowning laugh.

"And to exploration," Jan added in her funny accent that had no region to it.

John and Roger laughed with their heads together. Jan had known Roger for years; I'd met him once or twice before at her house. She said John was his lover, but Roger looked at her across the table as if he were playing the usual small part he had in movies, the ex-husband or the jilted boyfriend. With one hand on John's shoulder, he watched Jan and Ed try to twine their arms together while they raised their glasses.

I felt as though I were at a party I hadn't been invited to. I imagined Ed and Jan in Jan's brass bed with its velvet patchwork quilt. Ed leans to her as she whispers in his ear, then sucks his earlobe and licks his cheek and chin like a cat. She's slender and quick, so unlike bulky Fran with his dark beard and heavy tread. I couldn't picture those two in bed together, but it was easy to see Jan and Ed, their thin, long arms and legs wrapped around each other, Jan dark and Ed blond.

I spilled my wine. Jan jumped up to get a sponge, and wiped the table carefully while I dabbed at the placemat with my napkin.

"We could go down there tonight," Ed suggested. "Let's gather up all the candles and flashlights in the house and make an expedition of it."

"It's unknown territory," Fran warned. "No maps."

"Terrific." John stretched like a colt ready to race. He looked about nineteen. I couldn't imagine what Roger saw in someone twenty years younger. Ed's eight years older than I am, which sometimes seems like a lot. I tried unsuccessfully to picture John and Roger in bed. "Count me out. I'm afraid of the dark." I shivered.

"What?" Fran laughed. "Only five year olds are afraid of the dark, Anna."

"But what could be down there anyway? It's a waste of time."

"There might be gold," said Roger. "People did that during the gold rush, brought back lumps of gold and hid them in their basements."

"The bones of escaped slaves," said John. His pale blue eyes were wide. "Or the ghosts of slaves."

"1890." Fran frowned. "Keep that in mind. No gold. No slaves. Just a family house."

"Oh, you're no fun." John lifted the candelabra from the center of the table. It was a huge brass thing that held a dozen candles. "Onward!" he shouted.

Fran stood up. " All right, I give up. I'll get some flashlights."

Ed took my hand and pulled me up. "Please come, Anna," he said.

"Well, maybe." I could always slip back when no one was looking, I thought, and go upstairs to the library and read until they came back.

Fran returned with enough flashlights for everyone. "Put that thing back on the table," he said to John. "You'll burn the house down. Follow me."

He led us into the kitchen, and stopped in front of a low door behind the butcher block table.

Jan did a sort of dance, waving her flashlight in an arc across the ceiling.

"Let's take the plunge," said Fran as he opened the door and shone his flashlight down the stairs. The damp basement air crept around our legs.

"Don't worry, Anna." Fran ducked through the door. "You can stand up straight once you're on the stairs. They used to keep milk and vegetables in the cellar before there was refrigeration. It's just one big icebox."

Ed followed Fran, then came Jan. Roger and John held hands behind her. When I looked through the door, I could see nothing but the pinpoints of five flashlights below. Jan gasped and Fran laughed.

"Cobwebs!" she shouted. "My God, I thought some ghost had its fingers 'round my neck." Then she called to me, "Where are you, Anna?"

I turned off my flashlight. "I changed my mind. I'm not coming."

"Leave the door open," Fran shouted, "so we can see the light."

I left the flashlight on the kitchen table and walked through the deserted dining room and up the stairs to the second floor. At the top of the stairs was a framed black-and-white photograph of Fran and Jan's wedding, not when they got married in New Orleans, but the wedding they had in San Francisco when they were twenty-three and Fran's family realized they weren't just rebellious kids anymore. They stand arm in arm on the beach, Fran in a white tuxedo and Jan in a flowery lavender dress with long sleeves, the sort of thing women wore in 1966. Fran's beard blends into Jan's hair so that it's impossible to tell which is beard and which is hair.

Below the wedding photo was an enlargement of a picture I'd looked at a lot because Ed has a smaller print. It's of him and Fran and Jan sitting around a table with a red sun umbrella on it and a beach in the background, not the wedding beach but a tropical beach with white sand. They're drinking beer with labels in Spanish on the bottles, and Jan and Ed have their heads thrown back, laughing, while Fran's brows are pulled together. I know he's probably laughing too, but if you didn't know him, you couldn't tell from the picture. It was taken in Mexico just before I met Ed; he told me the three of them spent a week together in Mazatlan and planned to stay longer, but changed their minds. When I asked why, he shrugged.

I went down the hall to the library, a room with four walls packed with books, top to bottom. Two couches faced each other across a coffee table in the center. There were, of course, all the latest novels, as well as the modern poetry books Jan likes. Ed borrowed these all the time, slender volumes with paper covers written by people I'd never heard of, and inside each cover, in Fran's bold slash of ink, was written: *Fran and Jan Rose*. Even Fran's heavy law books had the same inscription that was in the novels and the books on travel and cooking: *Fran and Jan,* as though they were the same person.

"Looking for something?" Roger spoke directly into my left ear, and laughed when I jumped.

"I thought everyone was in the basement," I said when I could breathe again.

"It was too boring. You can't see a thing even with flash-lights." He squatted beside me. "They're all giggling about ghosts while Fran tries to be serious about history and beam structure. Here. The best books are on the bottom shelf."

He handed me a book of photographs. "This might interest you," he said with a smile.

The pictures all seemed to be of the same two women kissing and caressing each other, sometimes joined by a tall slender man with dark curly hair who looked something like Roger might have before his hairline started to recede. He turned the page to a close-up of one of the women with her head thrown back and her tongue licking her bottom lip. It was Jan, looking as if she'd just taken a sip of wine. I turned back to the picture of the man, and looked at Roger.

"Our first modeling job together," he said. "That's how I met her."

I turned to the inside cover, where Fran had written: *Fran and Jan Rose.* "It must have been interesting."

"Very boring," said Roger. "And freezing cold. It was in some warehouse in New Jersey in March. I thought I'd die. It took them a week, six hours a day, to shoot this. Of course, they only used a quarter of the pictures. It's all an illusion, you know. Nothing really happened."

I paged through the books to more photos of the women, alone and with Roger, and then to a series of Jan and Roger alone together, Jan with his cock in her mouth, Roger licking her but-tocks, and the two of them on a Persian rug, limbs acrobatically entwined.

I felt my face grow hot. When I bent over to put the book back, I noticed the other titles on the bottom shelf: *Women who Prey on Boys, The Story of O, Delta of Venus* — books I'd heard of and books I hadn't, but none I'd ever read. I pulled out *Intimate Sex Lives of Famous People* and opened it to Fran's signature. "Has he marked every book in the place?" I asked. "I'd hate it if Ed did that."

Roger laughed. "How well do you know our friends Fran and Jan?"

"Not very," I admitted. "They're mostly Ed's friends."

"It doesn't matter whose name is on the books." Roger put his arm around my shoulders. "Jan's the one in charge here."

I tried to shrug his arm off.

"Have you seen the view from the attic rooms?" he persisted. "Or are you as frightened of attics as you are of basements?" He dropped his arm, put his hands in his pockets, and smiled at me.

I wasn't quite sure what he had in mind, with John in the basement, not to mention his old friend Jan. I cleared my throat and said, "I've seen it."

The space between us grew, as though I were receding into a tunnel, an experience I'd had many times before while talking to a man who seemed to want something I didn't quite understand. To tell the truth, I didn't always like sex. I mean, it was the person who was important. Sex with a man like Roger who already had a lover just didn't appeal to me. Besides, he'd probably been Jan's lover, and maybe still was. In my mind I traced AIDS from Roger to Jan to Ed. Sex and death. I wasn't interested. I had made Ed promise to use rubbers except when he was with me, but I wasn't sure he did. I wasn't sure of anything.

"What do you want with me?" I asked. I laughed, and so did he as he went out into the hall shaking his head. I heard the stairs creak as he climbed. Maybe he did just want to look at the view.

When he'd gone, I went up to the third floor. At the front of the house was Jan's bedroom with the brass bedstead against the wall between two windows. Fran and Jan had their own rooms, though Fran's was more like a study, with a single bed made up to look like a couch. The third bedroom was almost entirely filled by a king sized waterbed which Jan said she couldn't sleep in because it made her feel seasick. I didn't know what they used that room for, since their guests always stayed in the attic rooms. I ran my hand over Jan's quilt, patches of velvet sewn together.

I thought that Ed and Jan had probably made love on her bed. I kicked off my shoes and fell onto the quilt backwards. The velvet tickled the backs of my arms when I moved them up and down. I pretended I was Jan, Ed's lover, nude on the velvet spread. The walls glowed soft pink from the ceiling light. I shut my eyes and felt like I was on a beach, on the sand, waiting for

Ed, my lover. My fantasies about sex were better than the real thing. Here I was alone and practically panting pretending to be Jan, but when Ed and I were together, something was missing.

It was awful to be thirty years old and know all about orgasms without being quite sure whether I'd ever had one. I think I was afraid to know I hadn't. What I felt during sex was more like a warm cocoon than a hot explosion. Ed was patient with his tireless fingers and tongue, but it was never more than nice, though I would have described myself as perfectly satisfied. If his climax seemed more like an ocean wave bursting through a dam, perhaps that was just another difference between women and men.

On Jan's bed I could almost hear waves, tap-whoosh-tap against the sand. But it was footsteps. Jan stood in the open door of the bedroom and asked, "Are you all right?"

I sat up. "Is the expedition over?"

"No," she said as she came over to the bed and sat beside me. "You don't have to get up, I just want to sit here a minute. Roger came upstairs, I think, but Fran and Ed and John are still poking around down there. Fran was right, there's nothing to see, but once I talk him into something, he won't quit. It's odd, he really doesn't like to admit I'm wrong." She laughed.

I turned over on my stomach and she stroked my back. I suppose I was still feeling the wine from dinner. Whatever the reason, I didn't move. Everything seemed unimportant except Jan's hand on my back.

She lay down beside me, rubbing my back, my rump, and then between my legs. Even through my pantyhose her fingers felt like they carried an electric charge. She stroked the seam of the pantyhose, pressing it between my legs, until there seemed to be a sort of electrical exchange, as if a spark shot from her fingers and went through my crotch and all up inside me. I gasped and immediately the word "orgasm" appeared in my mind like a word on a computer screen: clear points of light in darkness. That was it, so simple and so fast. The word disappeared, leaving a blank screen on which anything could be written. I was sweating all over, like Ed did when he came, and then I was chilled. Jan wrapped the velvet comforter around us. Another word flashed on my mind's screen: lesbian. I pushed the quilt away and sat up.

"I don't like women," I said. "I mean, I like women, but

they've never turned me on sexually. I never felt anything like that before."

"I thought not," said Jan with a smile.

"But I'm not gay, I know I'm not," I said.

"Of course not," she answered. "It doesn't matter whose finger it is, as long as it's moving right. It could be the same with a man, or by yourself. Anna, don't be angry, but Ed talks about you a lot and I've tried to tell him what to do, but explaining without showing him how is as futile as bumping around in a dark basement without lights."

I slid off the bed and put my shoes back on. "You do this all the time, huh? Seduce boys, girls, whoever you can get. And all the while pretending you're doing it for our sake."

She laughed, which made me even madder. "Oh, Anna, don't look so worried. Yes, I do care about people: Fran and Ed and you, too." She sat up and pulled me back down on the bed beside her.

"You and Ed," I said, "you've been lovers for years, haven't you?"

She slipped my shoes off again and pulled off my pantyhose.

"You all went to Mexico together, didn't you, you and Fran and Ed?"

She sighed. "That turned out to be a mistake," she said. "I thought maybe Fran and Ed and I could make love together, we were all such good friends."

"Fran knows about you and Ed?" I felt hypnotized by the fluttering movements of her hands along my arms and thighs.

"Oh, yes," she said. "We both have lovers. But Fran — well, as you saw tonight, Fran is reluctant to explore, and just as reluctant to admit it when an exploration turns up nothing. In Mexico it was deadly, Fran forcing himself to be with Ed and me. He and Ed were such good friends, yet they were beginning to hate each other."

They were as distant to me as three figures in a comic film, laughing around the umbrella'd table. I wished Jan would be quiet.

"I took Fran to Paris," she went on. "We left Ed with a note and a ticket home. He understood, eventually, but I don't think Fran ever has. Oh, Anna." She pushed her nose against my arm, laughing. "Can you imagine making love with two men? It was great. I wish they could have loved each other."

"There's too much I don't know," I wailed as her fingers moved faster along my thighs. "Stop talking."

"I'm sorry," Jan whispered.

I heard a buzzing noise and looked down to see her holding a beige and orange striped tube with a round ball at one end which she rested on her hand while she twirled her fingers between my thighs and up into my wet vagina.

"What's that?" I gasped.

"A massager," she said. I felt its vibrations go through me from her hand while I hung, timeless, until thousands of pinpoints of light danced across my crotch.

"Anna," Jan murmured in my ear, "there's so much I could show Ed about you if we were all together." Her words seemed to drift in the air without meaning.

"Ed?" I asked.

"The three of us," she said.

I couldn't imagine what he'd do except watch, which made me a bit uneasy.

"I did suggest it to him once," she went on, "and he said no, he was afraid you'd never agree. Of course, that was after our Mexico fiasco, when you two had just started living together. But if he saw us now, how could he refuse?"

I heard thumping in the distance, and a door banged.

"Make him lie down," I heard John shout from downstairs. "Get ice."

"Someone's hurt." Jan sat up. "Thank God John's here. He used to be an LVN."

"A what?" I asked.

"A licensed vocational nurse," she answered. "Come on." She jumped off the bed and tossed me my pantyhose.

When we got to the kitchen, John was crouched on the floor with a towel full of ice saying, "Hold it to your nose."

"It's Ed," Jan whispered. He lay on the floor at John's feet.

"More ice," said John. Jan went to the freezer.

"I didn't know it was you," Fran said. "I thought you'd gone upstairs. I heard someone behind me and I didn't know who it was, so I punched him. Jesus, I'm sorry." He rubbed his hands together like he was washing them.

"Can you sit up?" John asked Ed. "Sit up and tilt your head back. Hold the ice under your nose, like this."

Jan knelt beside John.

"I think it's stopping," said John. "Ed? How do you feel?"

"I don't know." Ed sounded like he had a head cold. "My nose hurts. And my head."

"We should call a doctor," John said. "If you were unconscious we should have you checked." His youth must have been an act; there were lines around his eyes. He seemed much older than nineteen now. "He was able to walk upstairs, kind of leaning on Fran," he said to me. "But he wasn't real coherent at first, and Fran said he was out cold. Fran was terrified."

"Fran didn't knock me out." Ed sat up, then slowly stood, leaning on a kitchen chair. "I'm O.K."

John felt his nose. "Well, I'd call a doctor, but if you don't want to, that's your business."

"Anna and I will take him upstairs," Jan said. "Fran, help us. We can carry him. You take his shoulders and we'll take his feet."

"No," said Ed, "I can walk," but Fran had him by the shoulders.

"Just relax," Fran said. "Lean on me. Let Jan have your feet."

Jan and I each took one of Ed's legs and lifted him from the floor.

"To the stairs," said Fran, and we carried him through the dining room and out into the hall, Fran in the lead walking backwards.

"Be careful," warned John, who followed behind.

Fran paused at the top of the stairs. We were all panting except Ed, who had his eyes closed and looked slightly gray.

"Where do you want him?" Fran asked. "My study?"

"No," said Jan. "On the waterbed. The door's open."

Fran backed into the room.

Ed groaned. We laid him gently down, and Jan covered him with a white fur rug.

"Where's Roger?" asked John.

"He went up to the attic hours ago," I told him. "Maybe he went to bed."

John left the room and started up the stairs. Fran stood in the doorway. "Do you want me to stay?" he asked.

"Not unless you want to," Jan replied. "We can take care of him."

Fran vanished, shutting the door behind him.

Jan sat down on the bed, and unbuttoned Ed's shirt.

"You look very pale," I said. "Are you sure you're all right?"

"I'll be fine," he told me, and to Jan he said, "Fran's finally paid me back for Mexico."

"I'm sure it was an accident," she said.

"Don't make too many waves on this bed," Ed groaned. "I'm still a bit dizzy." He closed his eyes.

Jan carefully massaged his arms, then said to him, "Sit up and take off your shirt so we can rub your back."

He sat up and slid his shirt off, then pulled his undershirt over his head.

When he lay back down, Jan rolled him over on his stomach. "Come here, Anna," she said.

I crawled slowly onto the bed and sat on the other side of him. We each took one side of his back and kneaded his flesh in synchronization, up and down his spine and across his shoulder blades, where I felt the knots Jan told me were tension spots, and learned to press them firmly with my fingers until they disappeared.

"Lower," Ed whispered, and loosened his pants so that our hands could knead and rub his ass. He began to move up and down until waves rippled out to the edge of the bed.

"You seem fine, you fraud," I heard Jan whisper in his ear.

"I'm much better now," he agreed.

When Jan slid his pants off and rolled him over, his penis sprung erect. His eyes were shut, but he had much more color in his face now. She unbuttoned her dress and tugged it over her head. I hesitated, then did the same.

Ed opened his eyes to watch us strip. The bed rocked like a boat on the ocean. "I see two women," he said. "I hope this doesn't mean I'm seeing double." He smiled at me. "Anna, I never thought you would."

"Oh, you hardly know Anna at all." Jan opened a drawer in the base of the waterbed and reached in.

"You don't, you know," I agreed.

She took out a small plastic packet and tore it with her teeth, sucking something into her mouth, then took Ed's penis in her mouth. I watched as though I were a spy. I couldn't believe I was in the same room with them. While Jan's jaws worked up and down on his cock, Ed writhed and moaned beneath her. Suddenly she sat up, removing the pink rubber sheath from his penis with her teeth. His fluid burst from him in a white foam that shot higher than I ever imagined it could, landing in a puddle between his thighs. Jan pulled a brown velvet cloth out from under Ed's legs, rolled it up, and dropped it over the side of the bed. Then she leaned over to kiss me. She tasted like a rubber nipple.

Ed was still breathing heavily. He sat up and leaned against the wall at the head of the bed while Jan pushed me back so that I lay beside him. She began to feel between my legs with her quick fingers until I almost felt a flash, then she stopped and, taking Ed's hand, guided his fingers to me. The two of them bent over me.

"Take your hand like this, across," she told him. "Gentler. This is how she likes it, she's different from me. Like this."

When I moaned and moved my hips, waves splashed beneath me. Slowly the ocean grew until it foamed up inside me. I heard myself scream far away.

"God," said Ed. "I've never seen her do that before."

Jan laughed. They lay on either side of me. We heard footsteps in the hall and then Fran opened the door and stood holding the door knob.

"It's late," he said. "Are you going to spend the night?"

"They'll stay," said Jan. "Ed needs to rest. We should leave them alone. She got off the bed and covered us with the fur. "Come," she said to Fran. She took his hand and led him away, shutting the door behind her.

"Well," I started to say, but Ed interrupted me with a kiss. Though I'd known him for years, I realized I'd never known him very well.

"Let's get under the covers," he said, pulling down the blue paisley spread. The sheets had a pattern of blue and green waves; it was like crawling into warm, smooth surf. He took another packet from the waterbed and sheathed his erect cock in glimmering pink.

"We've never done it with a rubber," he said. "Jan likes them a lot. She says men feel harder when they wear them, and smoother. What do you think?"

I didn't feel like admitting I'd never used one, since he'd probably assumed all along I'd been having other affairs; after all, that's what we agreed to do when we started living together. I took his plastic penis in my hand, feeling it with my fingers. It was like an alien being, a little Martian I wanted to suck up into the space inside me. I guided it in and as it slid up and down, I realized Jan was right: I'd never felt anything quite so hard or so slick. Back and forth, around and around, went the pink alien, while Ed's newly educated fingers danced across me and the waves of the bed threatened to drown us both.

"Blast off!" I cried, and the heat of a rocket rose inside me as we came.

When we woke, sunlight glowed through light curtains, revealing dust motes in the air. I sat up, but Ed drew me back under the covers and caressed me in the ways Jan had taught him until I separated and dissolved, my own molecules like motes of dust, every atom of me blown apart and recombined.

I fell asleep and when I woke again, Ed was gone. I dressed and tiptoed down the hall holding my shoes. The door to Jan's bedroom was open, the rumpled velvet comforter just as we'd left it when we ran downstairs last night. I put on my shoes and went downstairs. It was two in the afternoon by the clock in the hall, and not a soul to be seen. I found Ed in the kitchen drinking a cup of coffee.

"Where is everyone?" I asked.

"They left us coffee," he answered, waving a sheet of paper. "It seems that Fran and Jan are up to their usual tricks."

I heard footsteps coming down the stairs.

"Hello? Signs of life in the universe?" Roger called. "There you are at last, you've found my coffee." He refilled the cup he carried. "John isn't awake yet. You should try one of the attic rooms next time. When you leave the curtains open it's like fucking under the stars on a mountain top. I've been up since ten and I'm getting lonely. What do you think of our friends Fran and Jan taking off like that?"

I grabbed the note out of Ed's hands and looked at Jan's small, neat printing, which I'd seen so many times on invitations. "Fran needs to get away," she wrote, "so we've run to Brazil for a while. Special apologies to Ed from Fran. He trusts you to manage things at the office. There shouldn't be anything that can't be handled without him. Cancel what you can and and postpone the rest. Roger, stay as long as you want, and lock up when you go. We'll be back after Christmas. Love to all," and then Fran's handwriting scrawled across the bottom of the page as it did across their books: *Fran and Jan.*

"Just what they did to me in Mexico," Ed laughed. "When

you have their money, you can do what you want and hang everyone. At least this time they didn't leave me alone."

Roger laughed too, shaking his head. "They left me in London years ago, long before they were rich. Not only that, I had to ship their bags home while they hitched around Sweden together. I think I made Fran nervous. He's never known what to think of Jan and me. We both enjoy the illusion of romance, but the problem with Fran is, he thinks everything's real."

The day after Christmas, Ed and I received a postcard from Jan. "Brazil has done its work," she wrote. "We'll be home for New Year's Eve. Please come to our party and stay the night." It was signed as usual in Fran's bold slash.

"This time let's see if we can send Fran to Shanghai," I told Ed. I was finally beginning to know a few things.

Night Travelers

Angela Fairweather

Joanna eased her body onto the thick carpet of grass, adjusting her contours to the soft turf. Although the air was now comfortably cool, she could still feel the heat radiating upward from the ground, reaching into her bones. She took in a deep breath, then released it forcefully, allowing herself to be enveloped by the earth. For the first time in hours she relaxed.

She lay there breathing slowly and fully, letting go of the afternoon and all its problems. The children had bickered at the dinner table, a combination of heat and no naps. Her husband, red-faced and exhausted as he downed two icy gin and tonics, had complained about the stock market and how the subway always stalled under the bridge when the temperature rose above 80°. He had rebuffed her when she had playfully attempted to seduce him after his shower, pulling the towel from his waist and rubbing her body up against him. She both understood and resented his exhaustion. It *was* Friday, and hot after all. Maybe he wouldn't work tomorrow and would go swimming with the kids instead. Maybe they'd cook outside and sit in the dark together after the children went to bed. Maybe they'd make love.

Maybe.

Another deep breath. Her body became heavy, soft, pliant, receptive. The wonderful floating feelings returned. These were sensations she had discovered a year ago while lying in her darkened bedroom one afternoon during the children's nap time. She had not known what was occurring that first time as her body lay heavily on the bed. She had watched in detached wonder as she felt herself become lighter, bouyant, almost dizzy, and the air carried her until she saw herself lying below on the bed, her consciousness above it all. She had observed the softness of her breath, the eyes fluttering slightly, a half-smile on her delicate mouth. And then she had been back inside herself again, on the bed, looking at the ceiling, wondering what had happened.

She had tried several times to repeat the experience, but she had been unable to call it back. Then one night after calming a child held captive by a nightmare, she lay in bed wide awake, waiting for sleep to return. She felt her body becoming lighter and lighter, the sensation of twirling, of lifting, and again she was floating, only now over houses in the neighborhood, floating out toward the reservoir, over the deep black pines filled with the sounds of night. Slowly she circled the reservoir, then glided back toward town, toward her home, her bed, her body. She rolled over and looked at the clock. The entire event had taken less than five minutes.

In bed the following evening she had waited until her husband's breathing became slow and even. She had eased herself up, feet to the floor, gathered up her robe, and slipped quietly down the hall and up the stairs to her office. Settling into the old overstuffed chair, the light from the floor lamp flooding the pages, she had begun to read the books on the metaphysical that she had bought that afternoon. She had explored the mysteries of out-of-body travel: the realm of the occult, the mystical teachings of the ancients and of those more recently expressed. Her curiosity had been insatiable. She had guarded this time as she would a tryst with a secret lover. It was the only adventure she could claim completely as her own. She had decided to tell no one of her attempts to unravel her mysterious travelling. Her husband, she knew, wouldn't understand, or worse, would be concerned about her sanity.

Some nights when her thinking would become so complex

that it held sleep at a distance, she would force herself to concentrate on her body by sliding her fingers down her soft, rounded belly to her slightly parted lips. Slipping her fingers inside, she would pleasure herself until her back arched and muted cries caught sharply in her throat. Then her body relaxed and sleep returned once again.

As the winter passed and warmer weather returned, Joanna had spent many of her evenings in her garden. She would occasionally read there by flashlight, until the night she was caught by her husband, who had woken up and come down to the kitchen for a snack. He had called to her, first from the window, and then from the edge of the garden, his voice patronizing and bewildered. She had answered him jokingly, saying she had been reading a steamy novel one of her students had carelessly dropped. She had slipped the book between some papers she had been grading, then followed him into the house.

Later, in bed, she had rubbed her thinly satined body against his, teasing the edges of her gown lightly against his back. He had informed her gently but firmly that he had a breakfast meeting at seven and he needed his sleep. As an afterthought, he had mentioned that she should perhaps leave sexy novels to the young, who would benefit from them more than a middle-aged mother of two and a noted professor of history. Her body had stiffened and she had turned away. Perhaps *he* might benefit from some sexy novels to remind himself that middle age and a middle-class lifestyle were not deterrents to eroticism.

She had lain awake for a long time, wondering why they had married in the first place, why people chose those so different from themselves. She had known then that she absolutely would not share her new knowledge with him. The old feeling of resignation that she had experienced so many times in the last ten years had returned as well. A mild depression had settled over her and remained with her through the summer months like the pull of an old scar.

Now, lying under the August sky, Joanna began her travelling exercises. She imagined herself surrounded by protective light, a bright luminescence that would help keep her silver cord — the binding between her body and her spirit — intact. In this way she could travel outside her body without much fear of being cut off from it, unable to return to the material world. She evened her breathing, and visualized herself breaking free of the earth's pull, slipping up and out and into the netherworld of the astral plane. She travelled rapidly, whirling through space, losing all sense of time or direction.

She was on the edge of a meadow, lit only by the nearly full moon rising in the east and the thick mantle of stars overhead. The air was clean, heavily scented with pine and cedar. Somewhere in the distance an owl called; otherwise it was silent.

For a few moments she sat completely still, adjusting to the changes around her. Suddenly she realized where she was. She let out a soft cry of delight as she recognized the meadow of her childhood. Between this rich meadow and the rise above it, she and her family had spent their summers high in the eastern range of the Sierra Nevada. She sat in the meadow smiling, memories spilling over her: playing hide and seek with her brother and sister, fishing in the cold deep pools, reading novels, daydreaming, experiencing her first romance.

She chuckled. It had been a long while since she had thought of Shep. For years she had fantasized about him, wondering how it would have been if they hadn't drifted apart. Tall, blond-haired and brown-eyed, he had a powerful build and the easy gait of a young man at home in his body. He had been a junior in college, studing forestry, when they first met, and Joanna had adored him from the moment they were introduced at the rodeo dance on the Fourth of July.

They had seen each other every day after that. On the days he worked, she wrote long accounts of the night before in her diary, and dreamily looked after her younger brother and sister, waiting for evening, when he would be free to court her.

She remembered the first night they kissed, down by the creek where they had watched beavers building a dam. Although they were both inexperienced, when his lips first grazed hers, the sensation had been pure magic. Their first innocent, light kisses gradually gained intensity and passion. By the summer's end, they had begun a tentative exploration. Shep had touched her breasts through her blouse, then slid his hand inside, and finally removed her blouse to feel her full, yielding breasts, their small nipples dancing with excitement.

Two nights before she was to return to her family's home, their passion had overcome them. Shep slipped his fingers inside her panties as her body shook with excitement and fear. He took her hand and placed it against his swollen penis. She had felt the heat and tautness of him, the ridge of his glans pushing against the constraints of his clothes. He unzipped his fly and guided her hand inside, against the hot, delicate skin. The ache between her legs was incredible and she had wanted desperately to feel him enter her, to ease the strange pain she had never experienced before. But as he eased his body on top of hers, rubbing himself against the thin nylon of her panties, she had panicked and pushed him away.

Afterwards, they felt both disappointed and relieved; neither of them was quite ready to make that jump to adulthood. She cried from the tension, and from her fear of leaving him for home and school. He had comforted her, kissed her tenderly and told her he would marry her and take her home to the family farm in Tennessee as soon as he finished school. He gave her a gold locket, and she returned to her last year of high school starry-eyed and in love. They corresponded for a while, but slowly the summer became only a sparkle of a memory. The next spring her father sold the cabin and she never returned to the meadow.

The sharp snap of a stick startled Joanna back to the present. The hair on her arms and neck rose; her breathing became shallow. She sensed she was being watched, but she couldn't determine the position of the watcher. Very slowly she scanned the thick undergrowth. Nothing.

Then she saw the dark form of a man leaning against the trunk of a pine, as though biding his time, making certain she was alone. Terror swept over her. She fought to control her rising panic, to remain calm. She sat totally still, forcing her breath in and out as slowly as possible, trying to quiet the racing of her heart. She silently repeated a mantra over and over, on her guard as she watched the shadowy form. He remained still.

Joanna cursed herself for not having gained more control over entering and leaving her body. She remembered the books' warnings of the dangers of astral travel, of being endangered by unsettled and angry spirits, of breaking the silver cord and not being able to return to the body again. Desperately she tried to think of a plan of escape. She rose to her knees, then to her feet, keeping her body low to the ground. Then the man spoke.

"Please don't...don't leave. I won't harm you." His voice had a pleading quality, almost like that of a child.

She steadied herself. "Who are you? Why are you here?" she demanded. She needed to determine whether he was an illusion, part of the astral world.

He approached her with sinuous, light movements like those of a large cat, emerging fluidly from the undergrowth. Joanna was motionless, frozen in place, all of her senses alert, but powerless to do more than watch as he approached her. It wasn't until he was within a few feet of her that the moon emerged from the edge of the forest, creating enough light to let her see his face. Her body shuddered involuntarily as she gasped, "Shep! Why are you here?"

He didn't respond, but instead looked at her in an intense, half-starved manner, as if he could gain sustenance from her presence. The air crackled with tension. Finally he spoke, so slowly and quietly that she strained to hear his voice.

"I was killed in Vietnam in 1970. But I wasn't ready to die. Now I'm caught here, hanging in limbo; can't move on, can't let go. I've looked for you so many times, come back here, watched for you. Now you've come." He reached out to her, and caught her arms just as her knees buckled. He eased her down into the long damp grass, and steadied her with his broad hands, his arm across her back.

Joanna slowly tried to absorb what he had said. A more detached part of her wondered at the fact that his body felt as real and material as hers.

"Shep, I can't believe this is happening." She turned to face him. "You must have been so frightened, so incredibly alone."

He exhaled sharply. "My tour was almost up. I'd been injured once, shot in the shoulder. When I was dying I felt so angry. I guess I couldn't deal with letting go so young. I still go back to the farm and check on my Mom. My death was hard on her, it nearly killed her when they sent me back in a box. I went to see her a couple of times. She used not to believe I was there, but now she does. She seems grateful when I go to her."

Shep looked away. "And I've come here. I never completely let go of you, Joanna. I always figured we'd run into each other somehow, fall in love again. It's crazy, I know. But I've been waiting for you...."

Joanna sat still for a moment more before shifting her weight so that she faced him again. "I don't know how I got here tonight. I've travelled before, but I can't control where I go. I'm still part of the material world." She spoke as if to reassure herself that this was indeed true.

Shep said nothing. He extended his hand and gently traced his forefinger along her hairline, over her finely planed cheekbone to her delicate mouth. She smiled up at him.

"You look so young," she said. "I mean, older than when I last saw you, but still so young."

"I was only twenty-three when I died," he answered. "Just a kid. It's odd. I feel infinitely old but I'm still in this kid body." He shrugged his shoulders and grinned at her.

"You haven't changed much," he said. "If anything, you're more beautiful now. Your face has softened." He paused for a moment. "It appears that life has been gentle to you, Joanna. Tell me about yourself."

Joanna laughed softly, "Well, I went to college. In fact, I teach at a university now. I got married when I was twenty-five. My husband's a financial analyst, and we both worked for quite a while before we had our two kids, a boy and a girl. Oh, and we have a great old house that we've remodelled, and we live in a small town. You know, it sounds so perfect, looks so perfect on the surface. I feel guilty for even saying this, but I often feel lonely, and cut off, bored...no, maybe restless is a better word. You know, I have no idea how long I can remain here, and I really want to be here with you, to touch you and kiss you." She could feel her face redden at her boldness. He was looking at her, a smile playing across his lips.

"For years I thought about making love with you here in this meadow, how it would feel, how good it would be." She paused for a moment, took his hands in hers, and continued. "We may never have this chance again. It's what's most missing in my life. Intimacy. Deep, loving feelings and physical contact. My husband just isn't there for me and he never will be. I just...." She felt confused now, on the brink of tears.

Shep leaned forwards and kissed her tenderly on her forehead, the edges of her cheeks, the tip of her nose. "Joanna, how many times have I thought of loving you. I don't know how anyone could *not* want to love you over and over."

He encircled her in his arms, embracing her until they fell back gently into the grass, kissing long and deeply. He pressed his body against hers; she slowly rubbed her breasts against his chest, her hips undulating slightly, pulsing her pelvis as he began to swell. His fingers loosened the ties of her thin peasant blouse. It draped loosely, exposing her soft, round breasts, the nipples dark and hard, begging to be sucked. Shep's mouth grabbed one of them, his hand cupping her breast to his mouth, and he sucked long and hard with the urgency of an infant.

He moved back and forth between her breasts, first sucking one, then the other. Her fingers searched for the buttons of his shirt, working them open. They embraced again, hungrily searching out each other's lips, their breath coming in short gasps. She released the buttons of his jeans, with some difficulty because his erection was so great. She worked the pants over the prominent bones of his pelvis, over his rounded hips, muscular legs, ankles. Then she looked at him.

His cock was thick, thicker than any she had known, almost the size of her slender wrist. The glans was prominent, the ridge developed so that his penis appeared like an enormous, perfectly shaped forest mushroom. His hair was like blond silk, so different from her own, which was dark, tightly curled, and wiry. She dropped to her hands and knees, nuzzled her face against his cock, then caught it in her mouth, warm and wet against the smooth dry skin, the droplet of lubrication emanating from the tip. She pulled it deeply into her mouth, forming her lips over it, dragging them slightly to create friction. He moaned and thrust his pelvis forward, feeding her hungry mouth. Her hand caught up his balls, nails scratching slightly, then carefully massaging them, first one, then the other, then both together with the flat of her hand.

"Joanna, oh God, Joanna." His head was thrown back, his muscular chest barely covered with soft golden hair, the muscles of his belly in tight ridges as she sucked and stroked him.

When he could stand it no longer, he lifted her up by her arms and laid her back down on the grass, both hands caressing her breasts, down the curve of her waist, the flare of her hips, to the thin stretch of silk and lace that covered her.

He ran his tongue over the silk, smelling and tasting her delicate scents, the blending of her musk with an exotic Oriental perfume. She was already wet, so that her panties were soaked within moments of his attention. He lifted the sides of the lace, forcing the silk between the lips of her vagina. He worked the silk back and forth. Then he slid the panties loose and over her hips. She watched him, her blue eyes glazed. He kneeled over her, admiring her slender body, the soft fullness of her belly, the deep thatch between her legs. He lowered his mouth to her cunt, parted the lips with his fingers, and allowed his tongue to slip in between the lips, travelling through the folds and crevices he had imagined so many times.

Her body was bucking now, thrashing wildly under him, ragged cries coming from her throat. Her body was overtaken by great wrenching spasms, her breath a series of hoarse gasps. She pulled at him urgently, begging him to enter her, to fuck her hard and deep. He held his cock in his hand as he eased it in. He could feel the strain in her cunt as it slowly yielded to his fullness.

Joanna, eyes tightly squeezed shut, cried over and over, turning her head from one side to the other, begging for relief. Slowly, slowly he worked himself into her until he was fully embraced. Then he thrust forward several times, as the air between them crackled with electricity. "Shep, fuck me, please!" Her legs encircled his back, lifted up toward his shoulders, forcing him in deeper and deeper. She held her hands to her heels, pushing hard against them to create greater tension. Her breasts bounced wildly, not quite touching his chest. She could feel his body tightening, his cock stretching to its limits, then a great explosion as he came hard into her, again, and again, and again.

He collapsed onto her. Her arms holding him tightly, she kissed his neck, his face, his mouth. He released his hold and gently eased his body down next to hers, his arm draped across her ribs. They lay together quietly, breathing softly, his face nuzzled against her neck, resting against the perfumed tangle of her long hair.

Eventually they turned to each other, and talked softly. Her hand found his chest and began working itself over him inch by inch until it dropped down to his half-hardened cock. They began again, this time more slowly and completely until a waterfall of orgasms spilled over them.

"I think I can break free now, Joanna. I think I can go on."

She delayed her response, holding him to her breasts a little longer. "I think you can too," she said finally. "I've been freed as well. Oh, Shep, I'm so grateful for this night, for travelling with you."

"I'll be waiting for you on the other side, Joanna," he replied. "In our next life we can dance together more fully."

They dressed each other, and lay down once more, their arms encircling each other in a tight embrace. Together they drifted silently through the sky.

Joanna became aware of her body, stiff with cold, lying in the grass in the pre-dawn chill. Slowly she rose to her feet, feeling numb and dazed, coming out of a dream so close yet not quite remembered. Returning to the house, she noticed the tenderness of her nipples. As she stood in the darkened bedroom, silently removing her clothes, she was suddenly filled with a great feeling of warmth as the evening returned. Slowly, quietly, she eased into bed, stretching out beside the sleeping form of her husband, his body emanating a welcome heat. She placed her arm around him, pressed up against his hips and back, and relaxed. She wondered if her experience had been only a dream. Then as she slipped into the space between wakefulness and dreaming she was vaguely aware of a rush of wetness between her legs....

Among My Souvenirs

Marcy Sheiner

Five years is a relatively short period of time, and yet so much has changed with regard to sexual behavior in the last five years, that I find myself looking back with nostalgia at a bygone era. With AIDS running amok, the days of following one's desires of the moment are gone, at least for me and most of my friends. My boyfriend Jackson and I are staying pretty much monogamous these days. When we started using pornography to achieve the variety we had always maintained in our sex life, I remembered the journals I used to keep of our experiences, and dug them out to use as turn-ons. I found this story among my souvenirs.

Part of Jackson's attraction to me is that I'm bisexual. Even though we engaged in a threesome with another woman only once, he knows my desire for other women is always there. Like many straight men, he's turned on by the idea of lesbian sex, but he has little interest in male homosexuality.

Jackson is black, muscular, virile-looking. Women flock to him at parties and bars, and, although he says he's just being friendly, he is definitely a flirt.

Despite being clearly heterosexual, Jackson is intrigued not only by lesbian sex, but by the whole gay subculture and lifestyle. He's always wanting us to go to gay bars, male or female — something I don't feel altogether comfortable doing, since I don't want lesbians to feel like we're hitting on them. Also, I see gay men looking at Jackson as if they could eat him up with a spoon. And they look at me like they wish I'd get out of their way!

Jackson thinks that men are attracted to him because of his style. He always wears a sharp three-piece suit, or a spiffy shirt and sweater with impeccably creased pants. I think the attraction is his delicious ass. I'm convinced these guys are just dying to squeeze and fuck his firm round buns. I myself have stuck my fingers into his asshole while he's fucking me, and know the ecstasy of being inside him: the incomparable sensation of squeezing him from both ends, my cunt sucking the come from his prick while my finger gently circles his hole.

One Saturday night Jackson asked me to go to a popular gay disco. I'd been to the place with my lesbian friends, and knew that although the crowd was mixed, mostly gay men hung out there. I didn't want to go, but Jackson kept after me, implying that I was uptight. I began to question myself: why did I feel so threatened? After all, he'd slept with other women over the years, including once in my presence, and our relationship was still intact. He'd made it apparent that he had no interest in sleeping with men. And as far as lesbians thinking we were out cruising, I just wouldn't do that. We'd go to the disco, dance, and have a good time.

The disco was part of a complex that included a huge bar, dance hall, motel, and restaurant. The place is well-known in three states as a gay haven, although unsuspecting straights wander in from time to time. I've seen Frank, one of the bartenders, bring straight couples their check with the first drink, and then ignore them so they'd leave. Fortunately, he knows me, so Jackson and I didn't receive this kind of treatment. If fact, he probably assumed, as did most gays in the place, that I was a lesbian, and that therefore Jackson must also be gay. One aspect of being bisexual is that people on both sides of the fence assume I'm one of them.

At any rate, the bartender was friendlier than usual, making small talk while surreptitiously eyeing the delicious number I'd hauled into his bar. Jackson, in his usual naive fashion, joined the conversation, oblivious to the fact that a dozen pairs of eyes were riveted to his body; that men up and down the bar were mentally undressing him.

Feeling completely invisible, I decided to go upstairs where the dancing was, and leave Jackson to handle himself. Picking up my Bloody Mary, I slid off my barstool, unsurprised that no one, not even Jackson, who was deep in conversation with the bartender, noticed my departure.

Upstairs, men and women — mostly men — danced under strobe lights to the sound of Donna Summer. I sat at a corner table and watched the dancers, most of whom were moving in their own separate spaces, some consciously trying to attract attention. One man, wearing jeans and a purple sleeveless T-shirt so tight his nipples bulged through, was making erotic movements to his own image in the mirror. He held his arms over his head and undulated; he rubbed his crotch and moaned softly to himself.

In a corner of the room a group of women danced in a circle. They were dressed flamboyantly in purple and orange flowing skirts, their long earrings dangling. Recognizing one of them, I made my way across the room and joined the circle.

Dancing to the strong disco beat, with the lights flashing across the colors of the women's outfits, I forgot about Jackson and lost myself to sensation. I must have been dancing for about fifteen minutes when I noticed him in the middle of the dance floor with a man who looked vaguely familiar. He was doing his usual dance step, digging the music and the scene, but his partner was focused on one thing only: my man.

Should I be mature and keep on dancing, or should I go over and assert my rights? Convincing myself that Jackson might want to be rescued, I left the circle of women. As I walked across the dance floor, I suddenly realized his partner was Tony, a bisexual man with whom I had once had an affair.

Tony and I had never been in love, or anything remotely like it. We'd met several years ago in a small town where small minds were stifling both of us. We were so relieved to find each other in that wasteland, that we immediately began acting out our fantasies: everything from dressing in costumes to visiting the nearby city's sex clubs on weekends. Tony introduced me to the intriguing world of swingers, and told me all about the gay male scene. We shared our erotic writings with one another and felt a strong kinship as bisexuals. I never would have made it through that year without Tony.

Now here he was, my brother, my twin. When he spotted me, his face lit up like a light bulb. He left Jackson without a word and rushed over to embrace me. We kissed and hugged and stroked each other's faces. The music was too loud to talk, so Tony motioned for us to go downstairs. I hesitated, looking at Jackson.

"It's okay," Tony shouted in my ear. "He's just a number I picked up at the bar."

"Tony," I shouted back. "He's my boyfriend."

Tony's thick bushy eyebrows arched magnificently. "In that case," he said, a mischievous smile dimpling his cheek, "I suppose we should ask him to join us."

Down in the bar, Tony ordered champagne to celebrate our reunion. We sat in a booth drinking one bottle after another, and Tony regaled us with stories of his latest adventures, most of which held strong sexual overtones. He let it be known that he had a room at the hotel, and more than once touched Jackson's elegant hand while making eye contact with him.

I was amused. I'd seen Tony in action before. More than being merely amused, though, I was getting hot. I imagined Tony's prick in Jackson's asshole, his hand on Jackson's cock.

Dazed by the champagne, I barely noticed as Tony urged us into his room. My fantasy was coming true.

I sat down and lazily smoked a cigarette, wanting to be merely an observer. I knew Jackson was in the hands of a master. Whether with a man or a woman, Tony devoted the same degree of attentiveness and artistry to the object of his desire. I knew he had a fondness, as do I, for brown skin, and for muscular men. And here stood Jackson, my prize, a glorious man if ever there was one, with his well-developed biceps, flat belly, rock hard thighs, and an uncircumcised prick that was six inches at rest. As Tony removed Jackson's clothing piece by piece, I felt as if he were unwrapping a present I had personally delivered.

Tony was so different physically from Jackson that it was hard to remember they belonged to the same gender. A mere 5'5", he was thin and lithe, almost delicate by comparison. But what turned me on most about Tony was his face: huge brown eyes, full sensuous lips, big bushy eyebrows, and a thick mop of dark curls. He was smaller than Jackson in all ways but one — his prick when erect stood out a good eight inches. Now it bulged beneath his black bikini underwear as he finished undressing Jackson, who was casting questioning looks my way. I knew he wanted me to join them, but I signalled him to relax and let Tony take over.

Once he had Jackson naked, Tony began. As if wanting to familiarize himself with the territory before abandoning himself to it, he ran his hands over Jackson's silken skin, first kneading the shoulders, slowly circling Jackson's bulging biceps with his palms, then running his hands lightly down the chest. Jackson shuddered with pleasure as his nipples were gently stimulated, and visibly relaxed.

Tony sank to his knees and caressed Jackson's velvet prick with the tips of his fingers. He lingered a long time before letting his mouth venture anywhere near, while Jackson's breath grew more shallow. My cunt throbbed insistently. I removed my panties so I could play with myself and watch at the same time. By now the men were too involved with each other to notice me. My fingers rubbed my dripping pussy as I watched my man being taken by another.

Tony had all of Jackson's cock in his mouth and was greedily sucking, while Jackson stood, his arms folded across his chest. I could almost feel his cock gliding down my own throat, and I loved the sight of Tony on his knees for Jackson's pleasure. Just as Jackson's face began to soften, a sure sign that he would come, Tony removed Jackson's cock from his mouth and crawled around to face his ass. Jackson leaned his hands against the wall, and Tony licked and slurped, alternating between Jackson's huge balls and wide open asshole. His hand moved up and down Jackson's cock. They were both in heaven.

As Jackson began to come against the wall, Tony stood and forced his own cock into Jackson's asshole. Both men grunted and groaned, and my cunt exploded, aching to have one of them inside me. I was jealous, yet incredibly excited by their involvement with each other and their exclusion of me.

It didn't last long. Before I knew it, their hands were upon me, and I was being carried to the bed, where my hot pussy was licked by two extremely skilled tongues. I kept my eyes shut, so I never knew who was doing what, only that I came again. This time not only was a juicy cock inside me, but another was all the way down my throat as well. Thick come spurted into my mouth at the same moment it shot deep into my cunt.

Exhausted, we drifted off to sleep. In my dreams there appeared endless combinations of lovemaking between the three of us. Later, Jackson and I talked excitedly about the possibilities. For the first time in his life he was eager to make love with a man.

But Tony, always unpredictable, left for Key West. I keep trying to get Jackson to return to the gay bar and try someone else, but he's not interested. I think he's really hung up on Tony and doesn't want to spoil the experience by being with another man.

The next time we saw Tony, the AIDS scare had just begun in the gay community, and he was a changed man. He spoke with Jackson and me at length about AIDS, but since it had yet to hit the straight world, we thought he was exaggerating. Now we know he was warning us.

We look back on our one night with Tony with a feeling of nostalgia, and a sense of sadness for what might have developed had the fates allowed. We still find variety, though, by reading through my old journals, or watching videos, or reading porn. Of course, none of that quite matches the real thing, but it will have to do for now. We keep the home fires burning, hoping, like everyone else, that this too shall pass.

The Art Gallery

Jane Longaway

Perhaps the best thing to begin with is the pursuit. I had never been followed like that before and it had the effect of making me feel both frightened and excited at the same time. He was a big man in his mid-thirties with heavy dark Sicilian good looks and anxious eyes. His large shoulders drooped, giving him a sexy drug dealer look. I was looking at Alice's paintings which were so bad that all I could do was stand in front of each one for an agonized moment and then make my way slowly towards the next.

The man was following as I self-consciously went along the gallery wall from painting to painting as though making the Stations of the Cross. He was so close to me that I felt his energy like a dark hot river behind me. His body towered over me and leaned into me. I found it hard to keep staring at the paintings. Did I feel panic because he might be interested in me or because he might not be? I became confused and stupid counting backward from one hundred to keep a meditative look on my face. The paint had been laid thinly on the canvas, and I couldn't help but think that if only Alice had used more paint I might at least be able to study texture. The stranger put a hand out and gently placed it on my shoulder. It surprised me because it was a small fine hand with delicate fingers.

"Let's get some wine," he said in a deep, confident voice.

Too embarrassed to look at his face, I turned and stared at his black leather jacket. I was grateful for the diversion and for the chance to drink, so I followed him to the wine bar. I noticed that his feet, which were in blue boat shoes, were also quite small compared to the size of his body, and I found both his feet and hands very attractive.

We took our wine out on a little balcony and sat down on a plastic bench. I was careful not to sit too close to him, putting my purse between us and looking demurely at his feet. I was aware that the costume I wore was ridiculous and artsy, black cotton leggings with holes in the knees and a low cut white sweater cinched at the waist by a wide red belt. I had tarted myself up on purpose that evening to get my husband to notice me, which he did not. The man said his name was Philip, and he waited with his eyes on the little patch of white flesh on my knee for me to tell my name.

"I'm Nina," I lied. Ann seemed so dull.

"I like that name," he said in his low voice. "It suits you."

"Thank you." I looked up at his face and saw him studying me with a sort of rapture that made him even more attractive.

"I am an artist," he said, softly leaning his head close to mine. "I'd like to show you my work sometime soon."

"Oh," I said.

"I'd also like to fuck you," he added.

I held the glass to my lips and did not answer. I could feel the blood rushing to my face.

"I do watercolors," he added, and he started to roll a cigarette with his thin fingers. I stood up to leave, filled with a sort of terror at what he was suggesting.

"I'm here with a friend."

"Don't go," he said.

"I have to."

He sighed quite loudly and looked frankly at me. It was the look a hungry person might give a juicy steak. I enjoyed it. I looked briefly at his thighs which were straining his pants and imagined what they would be like to touch.

I shook my head.

He followed me back into the gallery where I attached myself to Virginia and Alice. Virginia, reeling with drink, was telling Alice what a genius she was. Alice just stood there pale and drained with a sad little smile on her face. When I turned around Philip was right behind me, standing back but close enough to touch. I grabbed Virginia's hand and squeezed it, asking her to leave with me, but she ignored me with a hazy smile and started in again telling Alice how brilliant she was and Alice stood there rooted to the spot, letting the words bounce off her.

I left the two of them and went to the entrance to get my coat. Philip followed right behind me.

"My studio is real close," he said.

I smiled but shook my head. He was looking at me with such frank sexual interest that I buttoned my coat all the way up to my neck.

He came so close I could see the gold flecks in his eyes. He pinned me to the wall with his arms.

"Why not?"

Was his desire contagious? I felt myself get warm, felt a temptation to ignore the gold band on my finger and pay attention to the intemperate stirrings of my nature. But torn between the possibility of pleasure and my duty I merely trembled in my heavy black coat. I couldn't look him in the face. I broke away without speaking and quickly got out the door and walked fast down the block. It was a cold drizzly foggy San Francisco night. It dawned on me suddenly that I hadn't brought my car but had come with Virginia, only now I was afraid to turn back. I was near Grant Street and could hear the buzz of Chinatown and see the lights through the haze. I walked toward it.

"Where are you going?"

I turned around and there he was. "Home," I called out over my shoulder.

"You live *here*? You live in Chinatown?"

I kept walking. I rushed into the first open shop I saw and hid myself among all the gewgaws and colorful junk. The store smelled of sandalwood and the damp. I looked at myself in one of the small plastic mirrors for sale and saw that all the makeup I had put on that evening was still there. My kohl-rimmed eyes looked pale and sleepy but the lashes were jet black and brittle, my mouth was wonderfully red and moist.

He came up silently behind me. I felt his breath on my ear.

"Let's go," he said. I turned and he was smiling wistfully. His delicate hands were hidden in his pockets.

"Oh...." I wanted to say so much but only "Oh" came out. I wanted to say that I didn't do that sort of thing, that I was not the pick-up type of woman, when it dawned on me that while Ann didn't go off with strange men it was just the thing that Nina might get into.

We walked out of the shop together. In the street he put his arm around me and held me close. He was so much taller than I. My face touched the leather of his jacket and my hair was below his chin. We walked like this without speaking. Once he pulled me into a dark doorway and held my face up and kissed me, sticking his tongue deep into my mouth and licking it slowly. We continued our walk to his place, silently vibrating with expectation.

His studio was small and poorly furnished, but there were paintings everywhere so that when he turned on the light I was startled. The watercolors were all of nude women, very large and realistic. The colors were brilliant and overlaid in a way that made the flesh seem to glow. All the nudes were postured so that their sex was pushed forward and each wore a whimsical little hat.

Philip took my coat and hung it up. He came back with a black straw hat for me to wear.

"Put it on," he said.

The hat fit tight to my skull and had three red feathers that curled down my neck and under my chin. Philip put his arms around me and kissed me, reaching behind to lift the sweater up, squeezing my ass with his hand. He moved his hand under my tights and ran his finger down the crack of my ass. I was sucking on his tongue and letting my mouth go slack and wet. He pushed his tongue to the back of my throat, then pulled away and told me to take off my clothes. I removed the hat first and put it on a table while he dimmed the lights and took off his jacket and shoes. There was a large futon on the floor with thick green and cream pillows. Next to the futon was a large brass church candle holder with a fat yellow candle. He lit the candle and the room was filled with a soft smoky light. In this light his eyes seemed black and as shiny as olives.

I took off my sweater and my bra, then pulled off the cotton tights and fluffed up my pubic hair with my fingers. "Come here," he said from the middle of the room. Hat in hand, I padded over the worn carpet in my bare feet. He took the hat and placed it again on my head, taking care to turn the feathers correctly under my chin.

"The hat is perfect on you with your black hair and pale eyes, it makes your skin like opal and your lips like blood."

He took a pot of red gloss and rubbed it on my nipples until they stood hard and erect. Then he put some of the gloss between my legs. I was already wet but his cool fingers with the sticky, sweet-smelling color made me all the wetter. Slowly, he licked his fingers, then put them in my mouth.

He was still wearing a soft cotton shirt and loose white pants. The shirt felt good next to my skin. As I kissed his mouth, my hands fumbled to unbutton it but he pushed me down with both hands until I was on my knees in front of him. He unzipped his pants and took out his thick short cock, nestled in a mass of brown curls and already swollen.

"Suck me," he said. He kept one hand on my shoulder while he guided his cock into my mouth with the other.

I knelt in front of him and with my eyes closed licked and sucked, making his cock grow thicker and bigger. It tasted like him, with a strong musky scent. I was getting hot. I took his cock out of my mouth for a moment and caressed my breasts with it. Philip was breathing heavily. He placed his cock in my mouth again, grabbing the back of my head and pushing his cock deep into my mouth. I gagged and tears came to my eyes. He pulled his pants down completely. His thighs were magnificent, huge, golden tan and as hard as stone. I ran my hands over them and kissed them in turn and then kissed the broad tip of his cock and his balls.

I sucked him some more. This time he let me do it in my own fashion, holding one hand on his member and licking the head and stem, then closing my mouth over the whole thing, taking in five inches, letting my spit make it smooth and wet so that it pushed into my mouth easily and sweetly.

Philip was moaning.

I relished his cock. While I was sucking on it I took his balls gently in my hand and played with them, resting my cheek against his hard thigh.

"Oh now, baby, we must," he said thickly. "We must lie

down, baby, or I'll shoot it right now into your pretty mouth...oh."

I let his cock out of my warm mouth and it stuck straight up, brown curls now moist around it. On the red flower of his prick was a drop of clear liquid that stood there like a tear.

Outside I could hear a soft rain begin to fall. It hit the windows, making the sound of fingernails tapping glass.

He helped me to my feet and gazed into my face as he adjusted the little hat, his fingers grazing my cheek as he arranged the feathers. I looked at his face but now it was closed to me, his eyes half shut, the full lips partly open in a rather cruel way. When he pulled me to him I could feel his prick prod against my navel. I wanted to say something special, but all that came out were little mewing noises.

"You really want it, don't you?" he said with great satisfaction. "I can tell by the way you sucked me that you want it."

Even saying "yes" to this would have broken the spell, so I continued making tiny soft noises that seemed to come up from my belly. My hands moved on his hard large body which I found so beautiful. I licked one of his brown nipples.

He led me over to the bed. Above the low futon was a picture that dazzled me. It was a large nude about four feet long, and the reclining woman looked a little like me. I touched one of my breasts and almost reached out to touch one of hers. Philip noticed my gesture but did not comment on the picture. He seemed to enjoy watching me look at it. Indeed, the woman who was lying on her side had grey blue eyes shaped similarly to mine with heavy lids. Her mouth looked quite like mine; however, her nose was much longer and narrower and the hair, partly covered by a veiled riding cap, was strawberry blonde.

Philip reached from behind and put his arms around me, caressing me as I looked at the picture. There was an expression in the woman's eyes that made me long for a mirror to see if my eyes were capable of such lascivious abandon. Suddenly I was lowered onto the futon. Philip crouched down beside me whispering, "Nina." The name itself excited me. I could smell him and could still taste him in my mouth. Now he was spreading my legs open on the bed and kissing my thighs. His tongue was thick and wet; when he started licking my pussy I felt for my own breasts and squeezed them. Although modest by nature, I found myself opening my legs wider and thrusting my cunt into his face. His tongue lingered on my clit and he licked at it until it felt so swollen and hot that I pulled him on top of me. He moved up my body, licking my navel and my nipple, then plunged his tongue into my mouth where I could taste myself.

I pulled on his curly dark hair and kissed his face and neck all over while he began to fuck me, placing just the stubby tip of his cock inside, and then taking it out. My pussy widened to receive it. As my hips moved to meet his, he rammed hard into me. The little hat fell off my head and rolled beside the bed.

He came inside me. My pussy felt every cataclysmic move. He stayed inside while I convulsed and creamed and clawed at his broad tan back. Together we lay on the bed, not speaking. I was looking at all the pictures in the room, dreamily expecting the women to step down from their frames and stand around the low bed, all smiles and warm flesh, rosy with pleasure.

"Nina, let me take your picture."

I was astounded. He did not say "draw," he said "take"; this disappointed me.

He jumped up and got a Polaroid which he aimed at me as I lay there. After a few shots, he asked me to stand and put the hat on. I looked at the hat and said that I would only put it on if he'd let me keep it.

Philip looked stunned and lowered the camera to his groin.

"In memory?" he asked.

Actually it was because I couldn't bear to think of another woman wearing it, but I nodded. He put the hat on my head and took his pictures. I posed for him, realizing now why all his models thrust their cunts out like that. His cock was hard again.

This time, with the prints spread around us, he took me from behind, cupping my tits with his hands and biting hard into my neck. On the floor were the color shots of me. He was so big that he covered me entirely. I placed one of his hands between my legs and he massaged my clit until I came; then, taking his cock out of my pussy he put it into my mouth and I took his pleasure into me, caressing his hard balls until he groaned and shot the thickest, most salty juice down my throat.

It was late when I got home, and I was surprised to find Jon waiting up for me in the living room. He looked me over carefully, taking in the little hat that I wore proudly on my head.

"How was that show, Annie?"

"Wonderful," I answered as I looked at my reflection in the hall mirror. My makeup was for the most part gone but my face was glowing and my eyes looked more intense, like they had the shadow of secrets in them.

Jon put his book down and drummed his fingers together. "Where did you get that hat?"

"It's a long story," I said. I took it carefully off and admired it in my hand.

Other volumes in the *Herotica*® series

Licensed to Plume

Herotica 2, Susie Bright and Joani Blank, editors (1991)

Herotica 3, Susie Bright, editor (1994)

Herotica 4, Marcy Sheiner, editor (1996)

Herotica 5, Marcy Sheiner, editor (1998)

Audio editions licensed to Passion Press

Herotica

Herotica 2

Herotica 3

Herotica 4 (due in 1999)

All titles are available from your favorite bookstore, or by calling (800) 289-8423.

Afterword

Herotica celebrates its tenth birthday this year — and I celebrate my fortieth. It's funny, I think of myself as a teenager when I first put together this original collection with publisher Joani Blank, but clearly the math shows I was no spring chicken.

I don't think any of the authors in our first book was particularly young or nubile. Like most women of our generation, we had become bold about our sexual interests because of our involvement in women's liberation, and because of the feminists who had articulated the power of the clit — the untapped and often censored potential of women's erotic imagination. We were the kind of people who had been revolutionized by *The Hite Report*, treasured copies of Nancy Friday's fantasy books by our bedside, learned our masturbation mantras at the knee of Betty Dodson, and perhaps even colored in an entire glorious copy of Tee Corinne's *Cunt Coloring Book*. There weren't a lot of uppity women who included sexual liberation at the top of their feminist politics at the time, but those who did were the wellspring of inspiration for *Herotica*.

Joani Blank's feminist vibrator boutique, Good Vibrations, was actually the oasis where we all came together. I worked, along with Joani and a couple of other women, at a small shop in the heart of San Francisco's Mission district. Joani's philosophy was not focused so much on the bottom line as it was towards sex education. For the women who visited us each day, it was a grooving of the mind and body on the topic of "What Women Want." Our customers were thrilled to learn the ins and outs of orgasm, and we had plenty to offer them in the physical expertise department. We also had lots of resources when it came to answering some of the most vexing and hesitant questions people have about sexual performance.

But about arousal in its most elementary form — the erotic inspiration of our minds? There was *nothing*, I mean *nothing*, on the erotic literature front that:

» came from a woman's point of view,
» had been written in the current half of the century (sorry, Anaïs Nin), and
» was unapologetic, unpsychoanalyzed, tell-it-like-it-is storytelling.

At the time, the computer revolution was beginning to produce the first 'zines that flaunted a take-no-excuses approach to women's sexual desire. *On Our Backs*, the entertainment magazine for the adventurous lesbian (where I was a founding editor) was one of the pioneers. I could see from the sales of underground rags like *O.O.B.* and others that there were plenty of women who wanted to read a female point of view on sex on a regular basis!

Despite the many naysayers Joani and I encountered, we were inundated with praise from the everyday women who came into the store and bought everything we had on our tiny bookshelf. We could see that there were an awful lot of readers who were being rendered invisible by the status quo.

Herotica is the living embodiment of the children's story about "The Little Engine That Could." We were full of good will, "candy and toys," but when we asked the "big trains" to give us a push to get up over the hill, we were greeted with nothing but disdain and rejection. It was Joani's decision to have her small publishing company, Down There Press — which had never done anything in the fiction arena before — take our idea up and over the mountain.

The fears we had, which we kept trying to put a brave face on, were generated by all the grave and punitive warnings that we heard from our peers in the publishing world. Commercially, there was "no market" for this; they told us, "women were not going to read 'dirty books'." It was as if we were ripping apart the whole virgin cloth of femininity by sluttishly insisting on publishing such a thing. Some of the bigwigs said they had no moral or aesthetic problem with our material, but that it was strictly for an elite — that ordinary women would be either indifferent or embarrassed by our ideas. It didn't matter that we were selling ten vibrators a day to "ordinary women" and that maybe they liked to read, too.

The feminist vitriol in our direction was not callous, yet it was nonetheless painful. There were a few feminist publishers who felt that erotic publishing might possibly be acceptable or "good for women," but only with the closest supervision of its content so that no part of it could be construed as damaging to the feminist cause.

What this meant in reality was that a "content" issue, for example, a woman who likes to fuck and get fucked, raised a red flag. When I think about it now, it amazes me that these feminist leaders, who were *so ignorant* about the ways of human sexuality, should take something as individual as female erotic pleasure and contort it into a sexist doctrine. They honestly believed that vaginal penetration represented a patriarchal plot to subordinate women. If you mistakenly thought you were having an orgasm from stimulating anything besides the very tip of your clit, well, it just went to show how pathetically brainwashed you were by The Man.

Objections and misapprehensions about the nature of women's arousal and orgasm are up there with the all-time fallacies, like believing that the earth is flat. And like other historical blunders, this ignorance dominated the public consciousness. Anyone who thought differently was punished and excluded.

The lamest objection of all came from critics who thought that only erotica with extensive and prescriptive latex barrier instructions should be unleashed on an AIDS-susceptible population.

What all of it came down to, apparently, was the irresistible temptation to "protect" women from sex, to tell them "how to have sex," to warn them of the dangers of sex — or to assume that if one never mentioned sex, women would certainly never get the thought of it into their pretty little heads.

Can anyone imagine having such inane conversations about whether *men* could stomach, be attracted to, or have the maturity to handle erotic literature?

The appearance of *Herotica* is one of the most important events in modern feminist history, because for the first time a group of women artists and activists faced down this travesty of prejudices.

Even though most potential contributors to the book had not personally confronted a room full of fundamentalist feminists, their awareness of the censure of our mission permeated the consciousness of everyone we talked to when we first sought story material. People were afraid to use their real names. They felt embarrassed by their hottest ideas.

Simply finding enough stories to fill our slender book was an incredible undertaking. *No* one seemed to know what a women's erotic short story was supposed to look like, how to begin, or what to write about. How did you distinguish it in a female way? We obviously weren't going to sound like Phillip Roth, Henry Miller, or D.H. Lawrence, and we wanted something more individual and unpredictable than a *Penthouse* letter.

Most women writers pulled a total blank when we asked them for story ideas. No well-known published female author would touch this project with a ten-foot pole (Anne Rice's delightful coming out as an erotic writer was yet to come). We were definitely depending on "amateurs," women with little or no publishing experience.

This situation continued through *Herotica 2*, our second volume. As editor, I was so desperate that I would walk into a room and approach strangers on the spot. Had we asked the bookkeeper yet?

How about my dental hygienist? Were there any women on the subway who might be possible contributors?

I thought of myself as a talent scout with a great path ahead of me, but it was clear that I was going to have to fill some pages myself if we were ever going to have enough text. My first erotic story, written under the pseudonym "Maggie Top," appears in *Herotica 2*.

I worried that if I used my real name in such a new genre, everyone would think I was trying to set the gold standard for what an erotic women's short story should look like. I blanched at the thought that my writing was supposed to be that great. I didn't want to be Exhibit A! After all, wasn't I just writing a thinly disguised autobiographical account of getting laid? How good could that be? Looking back, I can see how my confidence was as threatened as everyone else's. I've never used a pseudonym since.

You know, I really like my story today, and I tell anyone who mentions the book to me that I am, in fact, "Maggie." I have written several books since then, and I think I'm a better writer at 40 than I was a decade ago. But when I look at "No Balance," I say to myself, yeah, it still has the right stuff. It describes a real woman, not a fake doll blowing the pizza delivery boy. It has all the detail of a woman's arousal, and of her everyday life as compared with her fantasies. I can still remember how challenging, thrilling — and how arousing — it was to write the story in the first place.

The Little Engine That Got Her Rocks Off made her point. Nowadays, mainstream and small press publishers alike depend on erotic literature as part of their bread and butter.

The best and brightest accomplishment of '90s feminism has been its sophistication, insight and honesty about the reaches of female desire. Somehow our readers managed to both survive — and thrive — on a collection of passionate stories that didn't come with a warning label or operating instructions. And I am planning my fifth decade with more insatiable dreams than ever before about what a woman's future could look like.

— *Susie Bright, April 1998*

About the Authors

Isadora Alman, M.A., "Big Ed," writes a regular column on sex and relationships for the San Francisco Bay Guardian and has a regular radio show. She appears frequently on TV and lecutures on general communication skills. She has a private counseling practice in San Francisco and is the author of *Sex Information, May I Help You?*, a fictionalized account of her experiences with the San Francisco Sex Information Switchboard.

Emily Alward, "Visit to the Mighoren," is an academic librarian, mother of two daughters, and owner of two dogs. In her free hours she reads and writes science fiction. "Visit to the Mighoren" is her first venture into writing erotica. Born in Lafayette, Indiana, she has also lived in Maryland, New Zealand and Kentucky.

A. Gayle Birk, "Love Object," a raving liberal Scorpio, is currently working as a freelance writer but has been employed as soda jerk, file clerk, secretary and "even a writer." She was asistant editor of an insurance company magazine prior to receiving a research grant at the University of Texas.

Nancy Blackett, "Shaman's Eyes," is the pen name of a San Francisco Bay Area writer and performer. She wrote her first erotic story, "Omelette" (published in *On Our Backs*), at age 50. "Shaman's Eyes" was inspired by a dream she experienced after attending a workshop on erotic writing.

Khasti Cadell, "Workout," lives in New York City, where her life is ordinary but far from dull. Her habits include chocolate, ogling teenage boys and smiling secretly. A devoted creator of erotic literature, she wrote this fantasy as a gift to Lorna and Joan.

Cheryl Cline, "Pickup," grew up in a family full of dudes and pickups. Her dream car is a cherry-red '57 Chevy half-ton stepside, and her favorite heavy metal band is AC/DC. She lives in Concord, California, with her husband Lynn and their white Jimmy Sierra S-15.

Kathy Dobbs, "Read Me A Story," makes her home in Houston and works in animal care, one of her passions. She states, "Erotica being yet another of my passions, I enjoy being both reader and author." Her story is dedicated to Ginger, her inspiration and soulmate.

Angela Fairweather, "Night Travelers" has been writing since she was a child, and professionally for sixteen years, chiefly about education, health and food. She is married to "a very sexual man who enjoys erotica and enticed me into writing it for him." She has "a beautiful 15-year-old daughter who still thinks sex is a little odd — an indulgence for adults who haven't anything better to do with their time."

Moxie Light, "Police Protection," writes for several journals and periodicals and has written a feminist screenplay in search of a producer. She is the first woman to have taken a psychiatrist to court in Massachusetts and win.

Jesse Linnell, "Sex Education," first encountered erotic writing when she was 17, with a book called *Satan in Silk.* "Though the story intrigued me, I found its detail skimpy and its adjectives stale with repetition." Since then, she has strived to keep her details engorged and and her adjectives throbbing with anticipation.

Jane Longaway, "Art Gallery," is a writer, printer, voluptuary and mother of one fine son. She is known to go fishing when things get weird.

Edna MacBrayne, "Wet Silk," lives in a beach town in Southern California where she is currently working on a series of children's fairy tales. She is also the author of *Alida: An Erotic Novel*.

Lisa Palac, "Jane's Train," edits Magnet School, the first sexographic magazine. She defines "sexographic" as using a wide variety of non-sexist, non-violent sexually arousing words and images pleasing to both men and women to incorporate the tender and romantic elements of eros.

Charmain Parsons, "Affairs," usually writes horror and mystery stories. Although this is her first venture into erotica, she plans to continue in this much neglected area. She is married, with three children.

Jennifer Pruden, "Shades of Grey," is a newspaper reporter and photographer. She likes parasailing, marinated artichoke hearts and cats. She owns a ferret named Hedge and has been published in several magazines and journals, including *On Our Backs* and *Outrageous Women*.

Susan St. Aubin, "Our Friends Fran and Jan," is a writer with the usual alternatives necessary for money: teacher, file clerk, technical writer, secretary. "I'm overeducated, married, no children; I like cats, and I prefer to live as far away from cities as I can financially and logistically afford to."

Marcy Sheiner, "Among My Souvenirs" and "Work and Play in the New Age," is a poet, novelist and journalist whose work has appeared in a wide variety of publications. She sees the merging of the creative and sexual impulses in erotica as a primal form of self-expression. She recently moved to San Francisco.

Bonnie Stonewall, "The Sensuous Housewife," is the pseudonym of a woman-for-all seasons whose home base is a beautiful suburban tree-lined closet. A devoted wife, mother, grandmother, daughter, lover, friend and sex maniac, she is also a bisexual activist. Currently writing a semi-autobiographical book about women's bisexuality, she's determined "to make a difference."

Mickey Warnock, "Rapid Transit," a self-described lesberado from Hayward, California, spends her free time pencilling drawings of women's images, watching soaps and girls, going to rock concerts and writing — when she isn't working or riding the last car of Bay Area Rapid Transit (BART) trains.

Lisa Wright, "Just a Bad Day," lives in upstate New York with her husband and two cats. "My past experiences as a potter and weaver often find their way into my stories." She writes non-sexist fantasies for children as well as erotic short stories for adults.

Susie Bright, Editor, specializes in erotica and sexual politics. She has worked since 1982 with Joani Blank, publisher of Down There Press and founder of Good Vibrations, popularizing sex toys and sex information especially for women. She is the author of *Susie Sexpert's Lesbian Sex World, Susie Bright's Sexual Reality* and *Sexwise.* She is the former editor of *On Our Backs* and was the erotic film columnist for *Forum.* Since 1988, Susie has edited two additional volumes in the *Herotica*® series and several *Best American Erotica* annuals. She is the author of *Susie Bright's Sexual State of the Union* and co-editor (with Jill Posener) of *Nothing But the Girl: The Blatant Lesbian Image.* She has consulted on many erotic film projects.

To Order Down There Press Books:

Buy these books from your local bookstore, call toll-free at **1-800-289-8423**, log on to _www.goodvibes.com/dtp/dtp.html_ or use this coupon to order directly:

Down There Press, 938 Howard Street, San Francisco CA 94103

Include $4.50 shipping for the first book ordered and $1.25 for each additional book. California residents please add sales tax. We ship UPS whenever possible; please give us your street address.

Name

UPS Street Address

ZIP

Mastercard/VISA/Discover/AMEX   Exp. Date